May happiness come on secret winds and surround you forever in the ways of beauty.

Printed in the United States of America

First Printing, 2017
ISBN-10: 0-9977440-1-4
ISBN-13: 978-0-9977440-1-9
Cristo Morpho

Additional books can be purchased at cristomorpho.com or from createspace.com estore ID 6361856

About the Author—Photo taken by Don R. Whipple, Whipple Photography, Newport, VT.

THE COVER IMAGE

The artist, Luis Royo, is one of the most popular fantasy illustrators in the world. The name of this painting is Coyote Summer. He began his artistic career in the world of painting and comic books in the 70s. In 1983, he began his career as an illustrator, where he achieved his greatest successes, illustrating book covers for the most prestigious American publishing companies, such as Tor Books, Berkley Books, Avon, Warner Books, Batman Books, and others. He does many cases for films, bands, and video games. Luis Royo established himself internationally as a master of fantasy and science fiction illustration. He has remarkable skill for creating female characters full of sensuality and strength. Rights for permission purchased through Alan Lynch Artists.

RANDOLPH C. PHELPS

Swan Song

a love story
with a
native twist

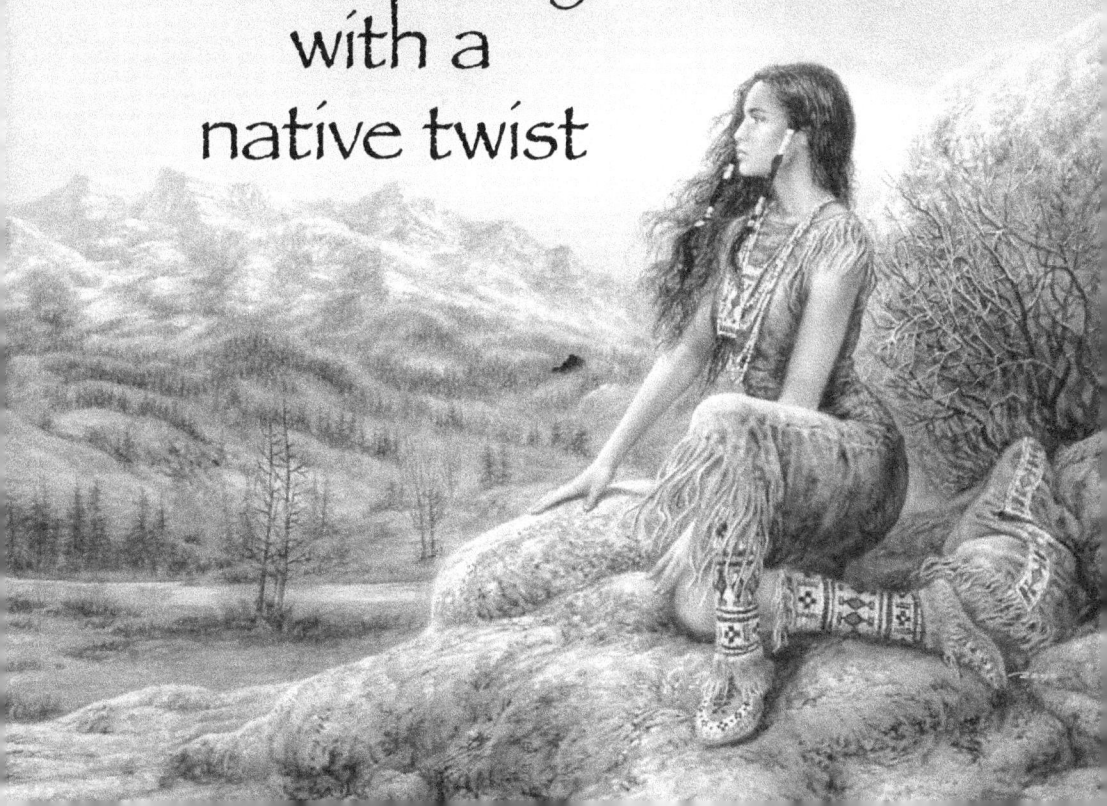

AUTHOR'S PREFACE

My story is the truth as I see it, carefully written with an awareness of sensitive topics. This book is not fiction. The events are real.

Swan Song is also included in the third section of my memoir, *Ten Minutes, Ten Days, Ten Years: Finding the Grace of God*. If you have read *Swan Song*, the first two sections are also available in a book called *The Cosmic Guru*. Both of these books include a final guided meditation that allows the words to fully absorb into the heart. The reader is guided to receive a word of wisdom, a vision, or healing. The meditation is intended for readers who have read *Swan Song* and *The Cosmic Guru* or *Ten Minutes, Ten Days, Ten Years*.

I dedicate this book to Swan Song and
to those who fearlessly continue to seek love
after their heart has been broken.

TABLE OF CONTENTS

THE CAST

I have given pseudonyms to the key characters in Swan Song. This allows some discretion, and the fun names reveal a bit about each person's distinguishing trait.

Cetan Luta .... Red Hawk

Wicahpi Ska .... White Star

Old Medicine Man .... Wicahcala

My Beloved .... Swan Song

Swan Song's Partner .... Chief Thunder Cloud

Teacher of Native American Traditions ... My Native Brother

Red Hook Internet Date .... Pandora

Past Life Daughter .... Feather Maker

Past Life Son .... Lost Son

Liberty University Housemate .... Cowboy

Omega Life Coach .... Nora Queesting

Omega Male Friends .... Eric the Viking & G. I. Joe

Omega Female Friends .... Sunshine & Terracotta

Omega Fairy-like Friend .... Blossom

Omega Akashic Record Reader .... Krystal Baal

Omega Meditation Teacher .... Althea

Althea's Husband .... Huck Finn

Sweat Lodge Friend .... Walking Bear

Abode Female Friends .... Izabella & Fascia

The Shaman .... Charcoal

My Dad .... The Lion

My Mom .... The Lamb

My Brother .... Gadget

Swan Song

The swan song in ancient Greek is a metaphorical phrase for a final gesture, effort, or performance given just before death or retirement. The phrase refers to an ancient belief that swans sing a beautiful song in the moment just before death, having been silent or not so musical during most of their lifetime.

Chapter 1

My Native Tribe

For over a month, I have had a series of dreams about a past life when I am living in a Native American tribe of Indians in the sky-wide plains out west. I am sitting around a fire circle with all my relatives. The smell of smoke lingers on my woven blanket. In the air it mixes with the other comfortably familiar smells: the dusty earth and pipe tobacco, a deer stew mixed with spices, wet dogs and horse sweat. Our tribe is a vibrant family. We radiate with love and warmth. I relate to each person in our circle through the blood that flows in my veins, a gentle touch, and a small, steady smile.

Nearby sits my sister's husband playing with my nieces and nephews. There is joyful light in their eyes. They smile and giggle. Our way of life is interwoven with nature. It is fresh, wholesome, and alive. We are grateful for every breath, every bite of food, and every relationship. Not just between the souls in our tribe, but also with the relationships we hold with the deer, the birch tree, the earth beneath our bare feet, and the sky above, where the blue jay flies.

My name is Cetan Luta. It means Red Hawk. I was given this name because I have a keen eye. I spot animals far in the distance. The red-tailed hawk is my totem protector. I honor it with tobacco, but more so with my respect, for it will swoop down and grab a rattlesnake without fear. I carry three red-tailed hawk feathers wound together with sinew. They are tied in my hair when I hunt so that I, too,

3

will be without fear.

I am returning from an afternoon of autumn hunting with my older brother and two other warriors. Up ahead, two trails meet and our paths will part. We stop to divide up our game. My older brother pats my shoulder and says, "Next time we hunt rabbits, you stomp on the pile. I will shoot them. Then I can go home with two rabbits." My arrow was deflected by a branch and one rabbit scampered away. I smile and reply, "Why do you need two rabbits when you have no wife?" He snickers and replies, "I will find a wife before your arrow finds that missing rabbit." We depart laughing. The path on the left is a shortcut to the river. I walk down it carrying two drooping, brown rabbits. The lush green tree line of the forest gives way to a field of waist-high golden grass. It blends with the color of my buckskin clothing with its hanging braided strands.

For generations, as long as we have known, the women have designed our clothing and sewn in the brightly-colored seed-bead design of the eagle. We also honor the eagle by painting it on the side of our teepees. It distinguishes our people from the distant tribes beyond the pine-scented mountains. I walk tall and proud to honor our ancestors. They taught me how to walk softly in all circumstances: from heel to toe when hunting, and by listening to every person around the fire before blurting out my thoughts. Many ancestors are gone. Now they live in the stars.

I bend down on one knee to clean my hands. Then I cup water in my palms to refresh my face and quench my thirst. I stand up and pause to admire how the golden grass waves in the wind and how the sun sparkles on the river. My eyes soften when I peer in the direction of the winding path beside the riverbank. It leads to our teepee. There awaits my wife and our two kids: my family.

My wife is Wicahpi Ska. Her name means White Star.

She was born in the middle of the night. An extremely bright star flew across the sky that night. Her brown eyes are fawn-soft. Her touch is tender, like a warm summer wind. During the day, she joined the other women to gather roots, berries, and nuts in the baskets they had woven. Both she and I have warm thoughts, anticipating our reuniting in the late afternoon.

Wicahpi Ska comes into view. She is gathering water farther up the river by filling up the preserved stomach and bladder from harvested animals. She is singing a beautiful Native song. I silently step closer so I can listen to her sing. I watch her with a soft smile. Her voice is enchanting. My heart beats faster when I am near her. She always dresses carefully. Today her hair is flowing wild and free, without any braids. When she notices me, the singing stops, our eyes meet, and her smile instantly fills me with joy. We softly embrace. She exclaims in our Native language how it is a pleasure for Cetan Luta to find her by the river. I respond in kind, flirtatiously saying the pleasure is more Cetan Luta's because now he is near Wicahpi Ska. She squints her eyes and smiles again. We walk back along the trail, with my arm wrapped around her shoulder. In her other hand she carries the pouches of water.

Our two young, brown-eyed children, a boy and a girl, ages six and eight, dash out of the teepee. They must have heard our voices. I lean my bow against the teepee and place the two rabbits down. I scoop them both up in a huge bear-hug. I let out a jovial shout, and my daughter shrieks back playfully. My son is pointing down at the two dead, floppy rabbits. I set him down and squat beside him to explain how we tracked the rabbits into a bush pile. Then his uncle stomped on the pile to scare them out. I make a funny face and stomp my feet. I slowly make the motion of pulling back an arrow, then jerk my hand around to point at the target. I make a *whish* noise as I open my fingers wide to let the invisible arrow fly. My son is amused. He mimics my actions and we watch him until an outburst of laughter envelopes us. In our tribe, we don't hold back the urge to laugh or cry. We learn the merits of hard work and know there is also a time to play. This is what it means to live and to die. We are like the changes in the seasons.

One day, during my dream, a great tragedy strikes the tribe. The women are crying and wailing around the fire. Wicahpi Ska is torn apart, distraught, completely beyond herself with screams of agony from deep within. I don't know the cause, but even I am feeling great sadness. Later in the next dream, it's partially revealed: a warrior had died. He startled a grizzly bear. It grabbed him and gouged his back. Its powerful claws killed him.

This same dream continues day after day until the time is right for the medicine to speak. When the medicine speaks, it guides me to go for a long walk in the woods. I cross over two brooks and come to an old logging path with tall pine trees on either side. Two chickadees are chirping high above in the branches. I look up at them. Two feathers slowly float down. I hold open my hand and they both land on my palm. It's a significant sign. Native medicine is in the air.

"Native American 'Medicine' is not the same as the modern medicine that we think of today. It is not a pill or a procedure or anything else that can be used to improve one's physical health. When Native Americans refer to 'Medicine', they are referring to the vital power or force that is inherent in Nature itself, and to the personal power within oneself which can enable one to become more whole or complete." [1]

MY DEATH SONG

I appear on a dirt road near an old white farmhouse. Behind it, there is a large, circular, back field that scales up the hillside. Floating in the middle of the field is an island of tall, striped birch trees.

Sadness for the death of the warrior in my dream still lingers. I am trying to figure out why his death is so significant. We feel connected in some arcane way. That warrior was close to me.

Suddenly, my eyes lock on a coyote walking down the middle of the road, heading in my direction. They usually run away. But something is peculiar about this one. He stops to stare in my direction. Perhaps this coyote can sense my sadness. I am not a threat and I am not afraid. He angles off up into the field. Then he walks a wide half circle and sits down on his haunches, a mere thirty feet away.

Now I am feeling even more sadness. It is becoming overwhelming. I squat down by a small pool in the brook. At that moment, I realize why Wicahpi Ska was so devastated. The warrior who died was her husband, Cetan Luta.

But, wait a minute! She was *my* past wife. It was *me* that died. I sense that Cetan Luta was my same age, in a past life, at the time of his death. The medicine has been waiting to reveal his death on the corresponding day.

I sense the whole tragic scene from my past life. It all happened dreadfully fast. I was following deer tracks into thick brush. The grizzly bear was startled. It came rushing toward me. There was no time to react or defend myself. I felt a sudden shock as it clasped around my back. Then it gouged me with its huge front claws. My life ended swiftly — too swiftly. Something was missing!

In a ceremonial manner, I take mud from the brook and smear two lines down the sides of my face. I begin to chant in a Native language. As I do, the coyote in the field throws his head back and begins a series of yelps, then he opens his mouth wide and lets out a high-pitched howl. A bush is lined up directly between us, so I only see glimpses of him.

I believe this coyote actually wants to join in my ceremony. A coyote will sometimes howl when they are alone and searching for the pack, but joining me is inconceivable. What an amazingly-bizarre honor to chant with a wild animal, especially a coyote. But I am too caught up in my chanting and feeling the emotions to be overly concerned with the coyote.

My whole universe is opening. I am in a surreal, dreamlike state. I have somehow overlapped another dimension of time. Every sound is magnified. The songs of the birds in the far corner of a field fill my ears with angelic voices along with a sweet golden harp. I am smothered with the smell of spring flowers. My vision is soft and blurry. It feels like I am in two different places. One is definitely not in this earthly realm. There is a timelessness. It feels like a curtain has lifted and I am in heaven.

As the warrior Cetan Luta, I never had a chance to sing my death song. I died too suddenly. Yes, that's it! I need to sing my death song. A death song is to take away fear and give courage when a warrior is facing a deadly situation, usually before heading into battle or during a severe illness. Maybe there are other reasons for it in the Native afterlife. This is what he needs. That is what he is missing! I start to chant Cetan Luta's death song in his Native American tongue.

While I slip into this microcosmic universe, Cetan Luta's soul finds solace. I believe this window in heaven has opened up on earth to allow his soul to freely pass. Now he can continue to travel, as intended. I am assuming he is on a beautiful journey back to the happy hunting ground. I can sense the presence of a medicine man entrusted to watch over Cetan Luta's soul. He is more than a witness. He is calling forth medicine to make all of this happen. I believe that he is somehow connected to that coyote. I can't see him, but I can feel him. It is possible he could even be... inside that coyote.

Broken Circle

A dream, a vision of the circle that is broken.
The wailing of hearts still rings in my ears.
The cries are not for me but for the love of life.
I watch a child pick a flower and smile.
I am in awe and give thanks for the keeping of my relatives.
For many years, many lives, the promise is kept.
Release the medicine man that is entrusted
to connect the circle once again.
When the stars are in line, the spirit goes forward,
overlapping the past.

Once I stop chanting, the coyote trots away to the corner of the field and disappears. I stand alone for a moment. I am absorbing all that has just happened. Cetan Luta's death song is a big piece of the puzzle. I slowly walk home. I go into the bathroom and look in the mirror. To my surprise, from the corner of each eye, wide, mud-smeared trails are streaming down the sides of my cheeks. They appear to be tears from Cetan Luta. They don't look like mine.

From this day forward, my dreams of the Native American tribe cease. But they continue in visions, and his past life continues to seek completion through cherished people that I meet in this life. Some of my new closest friends were, without a doubt, part of my past life within that Native American tribe. Our past and present lives will soon start to merge and the broken circle will be mended.

WICAHCALA REVEALS THE SACRED NAME

Months later, in a vision, I see my Native American tribe again. My Native blood-brother has taken in my wife and raised my two kids, as is the custom. She learns to love him in her own way, and he provides for her. But her heart yearns with a passion to be with her first love: Cetan Luta. When she misses him, she stands under the stars to feel his presence.

Wicahpi Ska prays with a pure heart to the medicine men for their spirits to be reunited. The medicine men live in the stars, beyond time and space. They look down upon their people to protect and provide for the needs of their souls.

Some Native Americans have two names; one name is never made public because of the power it would give another over them. The secret and sacred names are meant to only be known by the individual and the medicine man who watches guard over that person during life and beyond. Cetan Luta had trusted Wicahpi Ska so much that he told her his sacred name. It was Ohitika, which means "Appears Bravely."

One night, while Wicahpi Ska was praying under the stars, the old medicine man called Wicahcala appeared. He said, "Your heart is pure and your prayers are heard. The spirits of Cetan Luta *Ohitika* and Wicahpi Ska will be reunited." She was overjoyed when she heard his words. Only the medicine man that watches over Cetan Luta during his life and beyond would know his sacred name. It didn't matter to her if it happened in this life, or the next, or in the spirit world. She found hope and comfort in knowing that one day her spirit would reunite with Cetan Luta.

Chapter 2

Pandora's Box

I am searching an internet dating site to find my true love. After a score of horrendous dates, I begin to refine my Internet dating criteria. One day, I enter the keyword "yoga." Up pops one woman named Pandora, who lives in Red Hook, New York. We email and then speak on the phone several times. She is pleasant, intellectual, and funny. Eventually, we meet at a quaint B&B in Manchester, Vermont. We spend a charming weekend getting to know each other.

Before her arrival, I conceal several Rumi poems among the fields and flower gardens. Each has a clue leading to the next. We agree to be silent for our first walk. I lead her innocently to the first card. The silence allows us to be ourselves. We can accept each other without the clutter of trying to say the right words to meet some preconceived, self-imposed expectations. The final item in her scavenger hunt is a briefcase-size love letter. It is overflowing with sappy romance that shall never be repeated.

Later we walk on the mowed path that winds along a bordering river. I playfully bolt off the trail into the chest-high grass like an excited teenager.

Pandora grabs her cheeks and screams, "Are you crazy? You're going to get ticks all over. You'll catch Lyme disease!"

I reply, "Yes! I am crazy!"

I did not get Lyme disease.

We sleep together in the same bed. Neither she nor I want to stir up passion on our first night together. I suggest to her, "Let's draw an invisible line down the center of the bed and agree not to cross it." She agrees. I show her where the line is. I tell her, "I do not even want your little toe to sneak over to my side."

Pandora laughs. We both put on our pajamas and say goodnight. We each stay on our side of the bed.

Before I left my home, I had waded into a nearby pond and pulled up a pink water lily by the roots. I give it to her in the evening. I am a bit disappointed because it closed up. It was so beautiful floating on the pond. But the next morning it opens up brilliantly. Maybe there is hope for us.

The next week we discuss my moving in. It's not practical to date when we live five hours apart. We agree to live together even though we only met a month earlier. It's an impulsive decision, probably based upon the disillusion that we desperately need to find a mate to quench our loneliness. I pack my car and cruise down the interstate. I am anticipating that some sort of romantic relation will blossom.

I misplaced her directions, so I have to use my spiritual radar. I turn off on what I believe is her exit, then take a series of winding back roads that bring me directly to Pandora's lakeside home. It is a sunny picturesque day. She is standing outside in shorts with a cute halter top. She has red, curly hair down to her shoulders, and her cheeks are rosy and peppered with freckles. She gives me a big smile. I give her a big hug.

The inside of her nest is plush and cozy, filled with creature comforts. Friends often comment on the sweetness of her charming décor. She lived in Manhattan for twenty years and brought with her all the sophisticated charm. In the living room sits an ivory-colored replica antique chair with wooden ball and claw feet; on the floor is an entourage of oriental rugs, and on the walls hang several oversized angel paintings. Their eyes seem to be watching my every move, wherever I sit. There is a triangular-shaped, multi-level, gold-rimmed coffee table thick with layers of knickknacks from her world travels during her dance career. On the sofa and flowing onto the floor is a fountain of designer pillows in all shapes and sizes; some are silk with fringes. They never seem to find a proper home due to either their overabundance or their royal, flamboyant, flirtatious nature.

In the upstairs bedroom stands a flawlessly-smooth, dark cherry, sleigh bed with a pillow-top mattress. It is covered with layers of overstuffed down comforters and four pillows. Tassels hanging from antique lamps sway back and forth on each bedside table, and a huge picture window offers a nice view out toward the lake.

A few eccentricities catch my attention; one is what I consider to be a rabid gathering of what we both soon begin to call "stuff". Stuff is defined as bookshelves overflowing with new unread books, compact discs, and videos still in the cellophane wrapper. My assumption is that Pandora dove headfirst into mainstream materialism to fill the gap. Clearly, no man had been in her life for the last several years.

Pandora's zeal for gardening is evident from the rocks she has tenderly placed to resemble a serpentine coastline spilling out from the forest edge, complete with floating tulips, bell-shaped gardenias, and dancing daffodils. Her artistic arrangements rival those in Central Park. Pandora grew up near that park, and it is where her mother still lives. A statue of St. Francis of Assisi, holding a bird bath, kneels in an opening among the flowers. In his prayerful manner, he is calling out to the birds and squirrels. They are regular visitors each morning, along with deer that nibble on her plants, much to her dismay. She uses a little red wagon to deliver her compost and potting soil. This is when her inner child, dressed in overalls to keep away all the ticks, can happily play among the petals and bulbs for hours.

The first few days of living together are filled with the excitement of getting to know each other. However, by the third day, I begin to break out with itchy eyes, a sore throat, and a cough. My skin begins to crawl and confusion sets in. I am emotionally a wreck. For no apparent reason, tears stream down my face. It is not normal. Pandora thinks I am overly sensitive to what she suspects is mold growing in her home. I uncover that, prior to my arrival, she had thrown out green-spotted living room curtains and two pasty-green wicker bookshelves.

We decide to tackle the mold and merrily spend that evening listening to Barbara Streisand's Funny Girl as we scrub the walls, woodwork, and vinyl couch. Of course, Pandora knows all the lines and sings out, accompanied with the occasional animation from the Broadway show. With a new dehumidifier constantly sucking up gallons of moisture, we think we have defeated the mold. Unfortunately, the villain only laughs with a sly grimace at our attempt to fight an invisible foe with caustic chlorine.

Eventually, the mold compromises my whole immune system. I become sensitive to fresh paint, new carpet, and even dust. My symptoms progressively worsen. I decide that before I completely lose my mind, I had better move out. The mold eventually blesses all her stuff by laying a claim on every piece of paper, fabric, and wood. She refuses to leave her sanctuary, because it had been fine for the past four years.

MY RETREAT SPACE

I rent a spacious apartment in nearby Shakomako. It was an old train depot renovated with modern skylights, hardwood floors, and exposed beams. It has a history as a milk storage house for local farmers. Now wealthy horse farms surround the area and deer graze in abundance. I walk across the miniature covered bridge spanning a babbling brook out front. I have found my place of peace and tranquility. I call it My Retreat Space. I feel even more at home when I learn that this spot had been the wintering grounds for a Native American village.

A week later my reality is jolted. At seven a.m., Pandora arrives in a state of hysterics. She is dressed in her cherry-printed pajamas, banging on my front door with her cat in tow under her arm. By now, I am fairly accustomed to her emotional outbreaks, but this one is a notch above. She is babbling uncontrollably, coughing, and swearing.

She declares, "I can't...I won't ever live in that mold-infested house again. I awoke with burning, swollen eyes. I had to pry them open. I was barely able to move. I felt paralyzed. My legs were all numb...my fingers were tingling."

With wide eyes, I say, "Oh my goodness! Pandora!"

Pandora rapidly says, "I could hardly breathe. In a weak and dizzy state, I stumbled outside gasping for fresh air."

She was in a condition that medical experts call "anaphylactic shock." She should have rushed to seek medical attention. Instead, she comes to my sanctuary, with tear-filled sobs, and asks to move in with me.

At this point, I ask myself what good can come from Pandora moving into my home with her cat and all her toxic, moldy belongings.

Well, I cannot turn her away. She is my friend. I say, "Pandora, mi casa es su casa. You can stay in the spare bedroom." She moves in later that day.

We begin living together again. Pandora is sweet and charming as she dances and prances around singing her repertoire of Broadway show tunes. When we play chess and she begins to lose, the chessboard is suddenly shaken or she throws the pieces at me with a sassy smile.

We go on long, silent walks in the mornings. It's my favorite time to be with her, because the silence allows me to keep my sanity.

I tell Pandora, "You have ten chattering monkeys that live in your head, and silence will give them a rest." During our silent walks, I hold up the number of fingers that indicate how many monkeys I think are living in her head that day. She smiles and laughs at my nonsense.

I became close friends with Pandora, but it never blossoms into a romantic relationship. We never fell in love. There were no sparks. But she led me to an awesome spiritual retreat. That's where I find my tribe. And it was there that I meet my beloved.

Chapter 3

My Native Brother

OMEGA INSTITUTE

Pandora had worked for a spiritual retreat called Omega Institute in Rhinebeck, New York. Omega is a pioneering spiritual center that provides an eclectic collection of vanguard retreats. Hundreds of renowned spiritual teachers have imparted their knowledge. I dare say, just being there raises one's level of consciousness. When one stays for extended periods, such as the 150 volunteers, your "stuff" comes up. Volunteers and guests going through life transitions are drawn to this place, like children to an ice-cream shop on a hot summer day.

Before Omega purchased the place, it was a Jewish summer camp called Boiberik. It still retains that fun-summer-camp feeling; the kind you get when friends gather around a campfire with a guitar. It contains a beautiful lake with hammocks under the pine trees, a beach for swimming, kayaks, and rowboats. There is no better way to spend a sunny afternoon than lying lazily in a boat, chilling out, or chatting with a friend. I like to go to a spot called Turtle Cove and just float under the clouds.

Nature trails lead in loops up to the highest ridges. Scattered in the woods are a few homemade benches; nice places to sit and meditate. The trails cross over a bubbling brook and along the way you will probably pass by a few fairy huts made of sticks. (The fairies are usually bustling in the forest, but you can always leave a note.)

At the farthest side, near Kansas Road, there are several mounds consisting of hundreds of bowling-ball-size stones. They were thought to be ancient ruins from earlier dwellings. And I must mention the grandmother tree: she is near the sweat lodge site. She must be given hugs and offerings, regularly. It is an altar of sorts, decorated with necklaces, shells, candles, and gemstones. These little rituals are a big deal. When you're going through stuff, it helps to let go of something physical.

Omega does not operate during the winter season. The bonds created in one summer at Omega are strong and heartfelt. Hugs are the trademark at Omega. Even the coldest hearts soften after enough hugs. Everyone is accepted.... Gay or straight, young or old. If your hair is blue and you have seven body piercings and a dragon tattoo, that's cool! Omega is a place to experiment with different facets of yourself. Just let your love continue to flow.

At the end of the season, the volunteers say tear-filled farewells. Everybody gets one last hug and a promise to stay in touch as they exchange cell numbers and Internet connections. Half of the volunteers go to exotic places during the winter season and they rarely find the time to stay in touch.

MY NATIVE BROTHER

Pandora introduces me to a couple at Omega who specialize in Native American traditions. They soon become a major influence in my life. The guy I call My Native Brother is not a Native American (he is a dark-skinned Italian), but he instantly treats me like a brother. I consider him to be my first teacher of Native American traditions. His girlfriend, Swan Song has a beautiful voice. I cherish her as well, like a sister.

During one of our first encounters, they come over to my place to join Pandora and me for dinner. Upon entering,

Swan Song hands me a bouquet of wildflowers, along with a warm smile that fills me with joy. My Native Brother takes out two hoop bands of sage wrapped tightly in red cloth. He had used them in one of his past sun dance ceremonies. Swan Song lifts her brows and says to him discreetly, "Are you sure you want to give those away?"

He looks at me and explains, "These are sacred items. I want you to have them." He explains how they were used at the sun dance ceremony. I am greatly honored. My Native Brother begins to teach me, often through his actions more than his words. I can tell that his gift has tremendous personal meaning. That makes it even more valuable.

After dinner, My Native Brother begins to tell us about a medicine man he knows. He explains, "He is the great grandson of Crazy Horse. He recently went to prison and needs our prayers."

My Native Brother is a pipe carrier, which means he prays with a chanupa, also known as a peace pipe. He honors me by asking that I pray for this medicine man in my own way.

He invites Pandora and me to join them for a sweat lodge ceremony. It would be my first one. There is an inexplicable connection that occurs whenever My Native Brother, Swan Song and I come together. It feels like we have been together, as friends or family, for years. Our spiritual connection is unsurpassed whenever it involves the Native American realm.

My Native Brother mentions that he wants a rattle. When he speaks about it, my body tingles all over. I am inspired to find him a rattle. I search online and acquire a Southwestern artifact buffalo rattle that is used as a noise-maker in ceremonies and dances. This rattle measures fifteen inches long and is decorated with deerskin leather, beads, feathers, and flint. It is hand-painted and crafted by a Navajo artist, who has signed it.

THE ALMIGHTY ONE

The morning before the sweat lodge ceremony, I pray deeply for someone I don't know. It concerns addictions and letting go of past ways. Crows are flying around my backyard chaotically. I feel the spirits in the air. I leave early to help prepare the sweat lodge. Pandora stays at home. She is hesitant to participate, fearing that she will be sensitive to the smoke.

A few miles down the road, there is a gigantic, historical sycamore tree that measures forty feet in circumference. I call it "The Almighty One". On my way by, I spot a bald eagle flying toward the tree. It's rare to see an eagle this far away from the Hudson River. It's a powerful sign. I pull over to watch as the bald eagle lands on a branch close to the top of The Almighty One. It surveys the vast land beneath for a few minutes and then soars down to glide above the winding river. I notice a red-tailed hawk taking flight from a tree near the river. It appears to fly out from beneath the shadow of the bald eagle.

Around this time, back at home, a picture falls off the wall. (It might have had some assistance from Pandora's rowdy cat.) The picture is of a Lakota village, with a prayer at the bottom. Pandora stops to pick it up and reads the prayer. She takes is as a cue to come to the sweat lodge ceremony.

The Sioux Indian Prayer

O' Great Spirit
Whose voice I hear in the winds,
And whose breath gives life to all the world,
Hear me. I am small and weak.
I need your strength and wisdom.

Let me walk in beauty, and make my eyes
ever behold the red and purple sunset.
Make my hands respect the things I have.
Make my ears sharp to hear your voice.
Make me wise so I may understand
The things you taught my people.
Let me learn the lessons you have hidden
In every leaf and rock.
I seek strength, not to be greater than my brother,
but to fight my greatest enemy – myself.
Make me always ready to come to you with
Clean hands and straight eyes.
So when life fades, as the fading sunset,
My spirit may come to you without shame.

THE SWEAT LODGE CEREMONY

The sun shines down. The woods are covered with a thin blanket of snow, except for a few exposed patches. My Native Brother and I ceremoniously place the rocks that will be used inside the sweat lodge upon a flat row of logs that compose the second layer. The first layer consists of four logs equally spaced at right angles to allow air flow for the fire. It looks like a miniature log raft. It needs to support the weight of all the rocks and the fire without falling over. Prayers accompany the first seven rocks. We take turns by holding a rock above our heads with both hands to honor the four directions, Father Sky, Mother Earth, and the Spirit within. He uses sage to smudge the rocks and the inside of the sweat lodge. We carefully stack split logs on top in a teepee fashion a few layers deep. He offers tobacco to the fire, then lights the birch bark on the bottom ablaze. The fire burns for three hours until the rocks are red hot.

It is always nice to stand around a crackling fire. It's

not quite cold enough to see our breath, but the warmth feels good. While we're waiting, I give the buffalo rattle to My Native Brother. He opens his gift slowly. He says, "The lightning on the side is a thunder being. I have a strong connection with it."

Next we prepare the sweat lodge. The dome-shaped, willow-branch frame is about three feet high and twelve feet in diameter. The intersections are all tightly wrapped with faded red fabric. The frame was probably built within the last year, but still remains sturdy. Swan Song cuts an old carpet into pieces to cover the cold ground for flooring inside. Then the three of us cover the outside frame with more than a dozen wool blankets. We start down low and go around in a circular pattern. Rocks are used to hold the edges flat against the ground. The second layer of blankets overlays a portion of the bottom layer. It is pleasant for the three of us to be working together. Swan Song smiles as she works. My Native Brother is lively in spirit. He is definitely in his element.

My Native Brother assembles the door flap. One edge of a blanket is attached to a four-foot stick. Two ropes tied to either end of the stick are tossed over the top of the sweat lodge and secured on the back side.

My Native Brother says, "No light should peek through or our prayers will escape." He crawls inside the sweat lodge. We fold down the door flap. He taps on the blankets in a few spots and his muffled voice directs us to where light is seeping in. Swan Song and I adjust the blankets from the outside until it meets his approval.

Pandora arrives. She doesn't join us in the sweat lodge, but five other friends arrive who will. I meet Shawn for the first time. I have a feeling it was him I prayed for that morning. Swan Song produces a bag filled with colored fabric for making prayer ties. She kneels by the fire on an old blanket and cuts three-inch squares from red, yellow, black, white, blue, and green fabric. She spreads them out. We all take one piece of each color. She instructs me to place a pinch of tobacco in the center of each and silently say a prayer. My Native Brother stands aside, deliberately looking up to the sky, then down before he completes each prayer tie. His face reflects how each prayer is formed with a firm resolve. Then he wraps them up tightly and ties them all on the same string with three inches of space between each one. It makes a row of colorful prayer ties. I follow his lead. We hang them around our necks. Once inside the sweat lodge, we will drape them over the rafters.

There is a pit in the center of the sweat lodge. The dirt from the pit is used to form an altar outside, between the fire and the lodge. Upon the altar mound we arrange our sacred items: eagle talons, eagle feathers, a golden eagle wing, a bear-fur bag, and a piece of buffalo fur from the sun dance. A three-foot stick is jabbed in the center with a few necklaces and rings draped around the remaining short branches. The chanupa is cradled with the bowl on a fur and the stem resting in the Y of another short branch. Settled at the base of the altar is a deer skull, each quadrant is brightly-painted with the four colors of the Native insignia.

I am told there is a spirit line that travels directly from the fire to the altar and then into the sweat lodge. After the fire is started, this line is not to be stepped across during the sweat lodge ceremony. I visualize a multi-colored snake four feet in diameter slithering up a nearby ravine and down into the fire.

My Native Brother and Swan Song bring out their chanupas. They honor the four directions and pray to the Great Spirit who created this world. My Native Brother explains that the sweat lodge is like a clamshell. One hand of the Creator rests above and the other hand is below the ground, with us inside. The hot rocks will be placed in the center. He insists that we wear clothing to show respect, as if our grandmothers were sitting nearby watching us.

When anybody leaves or enters the lodge, they say, "Mitakuye Oyasin" to show respect. It's a traditional Lakota Sioux phrase, which means, "All are related." It reflects the inherent belief of most Native Americans that everything is connected.

Just before we enter, a grizzly, white-bearded, giant of a man appears. He introduces himself as Walking Bear. A small bundle of sage held on an abalone shell is lit. An eagle feather is used to sweep the smoke. Shawn smudges up and down the front and back of each participant. I stand with my arms out in a cross. The smell of sage fills my nostrils. I lift each foot to allow the sage to touch the bottoms. He motions for me to turn around to smudge my back side. When Shawn is finished, he taps me on the head with the eagle feather.

We enter in a clockwise direction. My Native Brother goes in first with his drum, then the women in their skirts, followed by the men in swim trunks or shorts. Shawn and Walking Bear remain outside to tend the fire. They will join us after they bring in the first round of rocks. They use a pitchfork to pull the red-hot rocks from the fire. They are carefully set on a shovel and brushed off with cedar branches to remove any burning ashes. Shawn slides the first red-hot rock inside the doorway on a shovel. Normally, deer antlers are used to grab and place the hot rock from the shovel to the center pit. Unfortunately, we have no deer antlers. Someone forgot them. The situation is discussed between the two fire keepers and My Native Brother. They decide to use the shovel. My Native Brother blesses the first seven rocks by touching them with the end of his chanupa before they are placed in the center pit. The blanket-flap door is pulled closed. We remain still for a moment, enclosed together with the glowing rocks in the center.

My Native Brother leads rounds of drumming and singing, and we take turns sharing our prayers. Swan Song sings a beautiful Native song. Her melody allows me to forget about everything, as if I am being held by the Mother of all Creation. Walking Bear is well-versed in his prayers. It all seems quite familiar to him. He even brought his own rattle, which he uses during a few songs.

Inside the lodge is the sweetest, darkest dark I have ever experienced. It feels like I am back in a womb. After water is poured from a wooden ladle onto the red-hot rocks, steam rises. As we breathe in, the warmth fills our breathing passage on the way to our lungs. I focus on the sensation of the heat. We begin to sweat and pray.

Walking Bear yells out, "Grandfather, it is I, Walking Bear. Hear my prayers..."

It's remarkable all the different names people have for God. No doubt, He hears us whether it be Wakan Tanka, Great Spirit, Grandfather, or Creator.

During the first three rounds, we pray for healing for our friends, family, and the earth. Prayers are formed in the heart, float out through the lips, and are released for others' hearts to acknowledge, embellish, and support. I believe our prayers are also heard by the spirit of the medicine man, who enters the fire and tunnels down the line past the altar to nestle in the hot rocks, waiting to receive our prayers.

During the fourth and final round, we pray for ourselves. They bring in fifteen rocks. It feels like my chest is melting. Every rug and every piece of clothing is drenched in sweat. At first, I gasp. My desire is to escape the swelter, so I get down low. Then I realize, it is better to just surrender and bathe in it. We are being purified by the sweat that pours off our skin and the prayers that come from our mouths. To be more explicit, we are sweating out our prayers.

When Shawn prays for his recovery from substance abuse, I am instantly aware that it was him for whom I prayed this morning. We really are all connected. Right now, we feel like one sweaty ameba. We have distinct prayers, but underneath they stem from our basic desires and needs for our bodies and spirits. We all feel similar emotions, our own pain and pleasure, and we empathize with each other. We are connected with all humanity, but with these eight women and men in this sweat lodge, I have created a memorable bond. I feel comfortably loved for who I am amongst these new friends. I have found my tribe.

At the end of the fourth round, the blanket door is folded open and rested on top. The moon has risen and the planet Venus is shining brightly. There is stillness in the air. While inside the sweat lodge, we hear the hoot of an owl. My Native Brother strikes a match and lights his chanupa. After saying his prayers, he invites us to say ours. The chanupa is gradually passed around. We watch as our prayers rise up toward heaven with the smoke. It's the first time I am invited to smoke and pray with a chanupa. It's a sacred moment. The best way I can keep it sacred is to keep this moment for myself. It is truly ineffable...one of those moments that each person will experience in his or her own way.

Chapter 4

The Native Medicine

One morning, after a fresh rain, I walk in the woods that once were the Native American wintering grounds of Shakomako. I spot ten deer in the field and locate a great horned owl's nest with fluffy white off-spring inside. I gather some feathers, deer bones, and stones that I place together in a circle to perform a ceremony. I chant in a Native American tongue as I dance around it. Afterwards, I squat down and close my eyes. I have a vision of myself sitting in a circle with some Native American chiefs and the White Buffalo Calf Woman. I use tobacco to honor the chiefs and then I make a request, "I want to learn about Native American medicine." They pass around a chanupa and when it's my turn, I take the invisible chanupa and inhale. The Native American chiefs are patient and talk among themselves.

One chief looks me in the eyes to give their response. "First you need to complete our sacred rituals."

In part, learning Native American traditions holds the secret to Native American medicine. If my request to the chiefs had been to become a carpenter, then their response would probably be, "First you need to build several houses."

The Lakota Sioux have kept their traditions and rituals active and alive. The sweat lodge, the peace pipe, and the vision quest, dominate as the most common rituals in this day and age. There is a sun dance ritual that involves four days of powerful fasting, prayer, and dance. It's physically grueling and demands hardcore faith from those who are invited to participate. My Native Brother has participated in the sun dance ceremony a few times.

Over the years, I have been guided through visions from the medicine men, the Native American chiefs and the White Buffalo Calf Woman. I have learned a lot from my friends involved in the Native American traditions. These nature-based rituals teach ways to get to know yourself through prayers and patient interactions with your Creator. The people I have met at powwows and Native gatherings have always been kind and warmly invited me to participate. Their activities include drumming and dancing, learning to track animals, sharing in a circle with a talking stick, or just listening to stories around the fire.

JESUS HAVE MERCY ON ME

Occasionally, I get the desire and guidance to chant a phrase.

One day I am repeating, "Jesus, have mercy on me." I say it out loud for one hour as I slowly walk up an old, winding, logging trail in the woods. Near the mountaintop, I stop saying it because my mouth has dropped open. On the path, staring at my face, is an eight-point buck skeleton. It is hanging suspended by its antlers caught up in a three-inch sapling. It's eerie to be in the presence of this deer skeleton. The ribs are intact and the front feet are dangling off the ground. It is loaded with a story about life and death.

I presume it was on its hind legs, feeding on leaves, when his antlers became caught in the fork of the sapling. The sapling is flexible enough that it can bend back and forth, but strong enough to not break. I imagine the insurmountable suffering this grand animal must have endured — the horrifying moment when the deer realized that its large rack was locked in tree branches. There must have been an immediate shock and a frenzy to break free — a natural desire to place its front feet back on solid ground. I imagine there must have been leaping, gasping, and snorting during its struggle. Any other deer nearby would have been distraught by its slow, gruesome death.

At some point, the buck must have realized that he could not escape. He was hung on a tree. His fate was sealed. Did the buck experience a moment of surrender and peace? Did the buck grow weak from the struggle and eventually starve? I imagine that even the tree, being alive, sustained some trauma. This tree had no intention of capturing this great animal and holding it captive until its death. Life sometimes grabs you like that and hands you over to death, without an explanation.

Then I notice coyote chew-marks on the rib bones. I paint a picture in my mind of coyotes howling as they surround this huge buck during the night, to tear chunks of flesh off his carcass. If the buck was still alive, he would surely have been in a panic. Perhaps the coyotes brought mercy. Either way, his flesh ultimately gave back to feed the circle of life.

All the scenarios of how the buck died flash through my mind, but the overriding thought is of Jesus. Remember, I have been chanting "Jesus have mercy on me" for the past hour. There are many symbolic parallels between Jesus Christ and this buck. This deer allowed me to empathize and come to terms with the suffering that Jesus experienced on the cross. They were both pinned to a tree, for no real reason, forced to suffer and give up their lives. Neither of them were crazy in favor of the whole ordeal. Because of their deaths, others lived more bountifully.

Jesus said on the cross, "Father, forgive them, they know not what they are doing" and "Father, into your hands I entrust my spirit." Although I am not sure that deer can forgive, I can assume it held no grudge against the tree or the coyotes. Granted, Jesus was willingly allowing God's will to unfold, while the Buck seemed to be an innocent victim of unusual circumstances.

I reach up and unhook the buck from the tree. I can see, touch, and feel the buck. At that moment, Jesus becomes as real as the buck. I place his body to rest on the soft earth; then I give a sigh of relief for myself, the buck...and Jesus.

> *"Later, Joseph of Arimathea asked Pilate for the body of Jesus. Now Joseph was a disciple of Jesus, but secretly because he feared the Jewish leaders. With Pilate's permission, he came and took the body away. He was accompanied by Nicodemus, the man who earlier had visited Jesus at night. Nicodemus brought a mixture of myrrh and aloes, about seventy-five pounds. Taking Jesus' body, the two of them wrapped it, with the spices, in strips of linen. This was in accordance with Jewish burial customs. At the place where Jesus was crucified, there was a garden, and in the garden a new tomb, in which no one had ever been laid. Because it was the Jewish day of Preparation and since the tomb was nearby, they laid Jesus there."*
>
> *(John 19:38-42 NIV)*

I could sense the compassion that Joseph and Nicodemus must have felt as they tended to Christ's body in a manner that showed dignity and respect after such notorious abuse and injustice.

The buck and Jesus were powerful beings, but both of their fates were held in God's hands. Here I am alive. Certainly, less influential and powerful than Jesus. Yet God cares and provides for all my needs day by day, just like theirs, until my final day of reckoning. Will I go out as a victim of circumstances or willingly go without regrets, forgiving others and trusting in God?

MOVING OUT WEST

My Native Brother has made some difficult decisions. For personal reasons, he made the choice to leave Omega. He decides to move back out west, far away from Swan Song. She will stay at Omega. She expresses with difficulty that she wants to be free from their relationship. As a friend, I witness a few dramatic scenes as their relationship is painfully torn apart. It doesn't feel like it is my place to explain the basic dynamics of their relationship. But for the sake of the story, I will share my perspective and what I witnessed, as their friend.

Swan Song and My Native Brother shared a deep bond of love for each other during the years they spent together. My Native Brother did not want to let go of their relationship. During the next month, he tried to control Swan Song's actions from afar by requesting that she not spend time with other men. To my astonishment, he mentioned my name specifically. Yikes! The situation became heart-wrenching for both of them. I believe that Swan Song wanted her freedom, but loved him, and she couldn't have both. Their relationship was coming to a bitter end.

I go to comfort Swan Song in her tent. She is about to call My Native Brother on the phone. She is lying in bed completely unraveled, hugging her chanupa and sobbing. It shocks me to watch her hold the chanupa (a rock and a stick) so close. I am learning there is more to the chanupa than its appearance. It seems better equipped to comfort her than I. Perhaps holding the chanupa and praying allows her to get in touch with her emotions regarding My Native Brother.

PAST LIFE CONNECTIONS

I made the decision to stay in the area and volunteer at Omega Institute for the summer. I set up an elaborate 12x24 foot tent site at a location near a pond a few miles away from Omega. I confess, one reason I made this decision was so I could be near Swan Song. I am becoming rather fond of her. Our paths cross again and again at Omega, as if we are the only two people living there. We smile at each other, and each time we meet, she fills me with joy. I feel comfortable around Swan Song, as if we had known each other forever. Our connection grows in a magical way that feels fresh and alive.

One bright sunny day, I am sitting alone on a stone wall near my campsite thinking about Swan Song. I fall into a vision concerning the previous dream I had of the Native American tribe out west. In my vision, Wicahpi Ska (White Star) and my real Native brother were together. He took in Wicahpi Ska and married her after I died, as is the Native American custom. At that moment, it strikes me: Swan Song is my prior wife, Wicahpi Ska, and my native brother-by-blood came back as My Native Brother in this life. This vision revealed the past life connections between Swan Song, My Native Brother, and myself.

I remember how after Cetan Luta (Red Hawk) died, Wicahpi Ska prayed to the medicine man, Whicahcala, for our spirits to be reunited. Her prayers had been heard and were now manifesting in our present-day lives. It is utterly amazing! My Native Brother and Swan Song are together, just as they were after my death as Cetan Luta in our past lives. The circle continues, except now in a modern-day scenario. My Native Brother teaches me the Native American traditions as he did in my past life. Then soon afterwards, his relationship with Swan Song dissolves. This explains why the bond between the three of us is so magical.

I wonder…*Could it be my destiny to reunite with Swan Song?* It seems My Native Brother knows something is going on between us. Could it be possible that the prayers of Wicahpi Ska are manifesting, unbeknownst to Swan Song?

KIDNAPPING SWAN SONG

I feel it is time to reclaim my past wife, given her modern day consent, of course. It appears that her relationship with My Native Brother has run its course. It seems she is now available. I go to Swan Song's tent early one morning during her day off.

In a playful way, I say, "I am here to kidnap you."

She is just waking up and is in favor of this kind of fun.

She drowsily exclaims, "You can kidnap me — after I take my shower!" She takes a leisurely shower, then I whisk her away to nearby Burger Hill. It's a Native American sacred site, so we bring our ritual drums. When we are together, it feels like I am being held in an eternal hug. There are many feelings in my heart that stir and swirl. We are like two innocent children playing in the field. And it's a gorgeous summer day with an azure sky and whispy white clouds.

She has the gift to feel the Spirit World. I have the gift to see it. Together, our two worlds blend seamlessly. When I play my drum and sing a Native American song, warriors appear in my vision. When she sings, she feels an outer circle of women swaying to the left and right. When we sing and play the drums together, then the men and women both appear. The men and the women come together to support and nurture each other. We share a precious moment and finish our morning escapade by praying with her chanupa.

SWAN SONG'S CHANUPA

Swan Song has a chanupa that My Native Brother gave

her. It's difficult to keep it burning when she smokes it. Perhaps it's because the stem is plugged and needs to be cleared out. She has put it off for many full moons, and the pipe continues to speak to her about it. In my experience, the chanupa is an extension of the holder, even more so if they make it. If a chanupa is received as a gift, the owner places their energy in it when they hold it, make an alteration, or pray with it. Swan Song's clearing out of her pipe stem can be symbolic of clearing out clutter in her life. I believe she desires to make her own decisions and stand as a woman in her own power. During most of her adult life she has had a boyfriend, so her decisions were made in conjunction with him. Sometimes this required a personal compromise.

We spend a weekend with some friends at Wise Wolf's home, talking about establishing a community on land that I recently purchased in Costa Rica. As part of our intention setting, we have a sweat lodge ceremony. Afterwards, the sacred fire continues to burn. Swan Song takes out her chanupa. It is the perfect time to clear out her stem. We go over the steps, then I squat down and sit on the ground a fair distance away to watch her. I want to give her plenty of space. This is the first time she has ever worked on her own pipe. She puts on thick gloves and heats a rod by placing it on red-hot coals. Then using long pliers, she reaches in and grabs the hot rod. It's important that she does all the work herself. I enjoy watching her kneeling down by the fire as she works. I have a small smile as I watch her. She is beautiful. I feel proud to be her friend. She emits confidence. She is the only woman I know that prays with a chanupa. She quickly pulls out the hot rod and inserts it in the pipe stem. She resembles a pioneer packing down his powder musket with the rod. She occasionally stops to inspect her work and peers through the stem like a telescope. Once, she looks up to notice how intently I am watching her. I receive a quick glance and a smile. But her focus is on clearing out the debris that is blocking her pipe.

As she is working on clearing the stem, it starts to rain. This is not that unusual. It rained while we were in the sweat lodge. She keeps on working in the rain. This is the time for her to dig in a little deeper, even if it means getting wet. Suddenly, it starts to hail. These are not aspirin-size snowflakes, but hail the size of golf balls, the kind that dent your car hood with a loud *ping!* During the hailstorm, Swan Song and I both run for cover under the roof of a shed. It's May 20th and we had been in t-shirts most of the weekend. Hail was the last thing we were expecting.

I believe magic erupted from her heart and the chanupa when they were both finally free to breathe. I am glad I was there to support her healing. It was a tender moment to witness her reclaiming her power. Miracles just happen when Swan Song and I are together. At the very least, something beautiful and unexpected manifests in nature. After the hail stops, the sun shines long, golden rays upon her, and in the distance a beautiful rainbow appears. We both pause and look up as an assortment of swirling neon colors race across the sky in a huge arching bow.

THE EAGLE HANG

I am disappointed to learn that Swan Song has not completely ended her relationship with My Native Brother. It seems to drag on forever. He has been living out west for a month. My Native Brother has planned to participate in the sun dance ceremony, and Swan Song is going there to provide her support. I hope that during her visit they both get clarity regarding their relationship. The ceremony could be his chosen way to let go of Swan Song and mark the end of their relationship.

During the sun dance ceremony, women wear dresses.

Before she leaves, I purchase Swan Song a traditional-patterned dress to wear. I love buying Swan Song gifts. But this one is also my way of sending him a message. I am waiting impatiently for their relationship to end. What happens next I regret. I inappropriately use the power of the Native medicine for my own selfish reasons.

I use My Native Brother's old sun dance hoops to connect with him on a physical and spiritual plane at the sun dance ceremony. I give thanks to him for watching over Wicahpi Ska in his past life and Swan Song in this life. I speak to his spirit to let him know in no uncertain terms, "I am back in the flesh and desire to be with Swan Song. I am praying that today during the sun dance ceremony, you will let go of her and make the final cut in your relationship."

During the sun dance ceremony, the participants dance for three days without food and water. They receive spiritual nourishment through friends that pray for them. The sun dancers must go beyond their physical strength and rely on faith. At a designated time, two ropes are looped to two pegs that are slid through two piercings on either side of a sun dancer's chest. The other end of the rope is attached to the top of a cottonwood tree. Traditionally, they dance toward the center tree and then pull away. On their third attempt, they use all their strength to break the skin that holds the pegs.

Another variation is to place the ropes through a loop on top of the cottonwood tree. Then men lift the opposite end of the ropes and the sun dancer is lifted off his feet. He is suspended by the ropes attached to his chest until he is either lowered or breaks free when the skin on his chest tears.

My Native Brother did this variation with what is called an eagle hang. When they lift the ropes, he holds himself suspended with his arms extended, forming a cross. He is not willing or wanting to let go. Minutes pass. Eventually, he bounces and flops to drop down to the earth. As I connect with him from afar, I empathize and feel fragments of his pain. My Native Brother loves Swan Song, and the hurt in his heart is greater than those two ropes suspending him in the air.

SunDancer

I watched, as you came out
Walking with your head down, tears
In your heart
Wondering, always wondering.
We sang you a song, the wind and I
But you did not hear
We sing together, always
But no one hears.
I watched as you came forward
And sat down
Looking, always looking.
I danced in your eyes
But you did not see
I waved my arms and waited
As my leaves rustled about you.
It was not until you fell
And looked up
That you saw me, heard me
And recognized me.
I am the SunDancer
My leaves, rustling in the wind
Are my songs
The sun and the moon
My eyes.
It was not until you
Found me and
Acknowledged me

That you gave me life.
I am the SunDancer
I dance in the sun.

    @Wayne Scott of Swan Lake First Reserve of Manitoba, Canada

Chapter 5

The Melodrama

I arrange to pick up Swan Song at the airport after she has been away for over a week. She shares with me the details of the sun dance. I surmise he finally let go of her. Even though I still have amorous feelings toward Swan Song, my life has taken an unexpected turn.

Once Swan Song had left, I began to hang out more with an endearing, fun woman who is 20 years younger than I. Swan Song had been all excited about introducing her to me. One day, she insisted that I go to the art room. She went in and told her friend, who came to meet me on the porch. Her adorable companion stood in the doorway and swayed as we spoke. She was as cute as a kitten. One could not help but want to hold her close. When we are together there is a lot of warm bliss in the air. It is fresh and exciting. She is innocent and wise beyond her age. I call her Feather Maker because she is always making gifts with feathers dangling down to give away to friends. She and her gifts are filled with love. She is Asian with long, black hair and a wide smile. Her voice is husky, and when she ends a sentence, she lifts it up a note. I find that appealing.

So we start to hang out in her tiny tent. She keeps it really neat and clean. There are white plastic bins for all her clothes. She likes to burn incense on her altar. She made a glittery, celestial mobile that hangs in the middle of the trail at the intersection leading to her entrance. One needs to bow down to pass under it. She planned it that way so any visitors will honor her home. She has a single bed with a cushy comforter. One evening we ended up side by side, cuddling on her small bed. That part was unexpected. But it felt really nice for both of us. She has no barriers and is not in a relationship, so I spent the night. We both enjoyed being held and sharing intimacy.

It has been ten years since my divorce, and for the first time, I find the courage to open my heart. Perhaps because she is a younger, playful woman. She walks holding my pinkie, and at those times it feels like she is my long-lost daughter. She had a heart operation as a baby. It is as if her heart has stayed open since that day. One day, she was across the field and looked my way with love overflowing from her heart. I could feel the burn. She has a lot of love to offer, not just for me but for everybody. She wants to be a nurse, which suits her well. She is compassionate and upbeat.

Feather Maker and I often go to be with Swan Song in her big, cozy tent. Another friend, Lost Son, occasionally joins us as we sing songs, share our day, or pick out a card from her animal or Native medicine deck. When Swan Song and Feather Maker are together, they curl up like two kittens. I find it a pretty laid back and comfortable scene. Sometimes we all hang out in our pajamas. When the four of us are together, it is like we are a family again. Maybe in some bizarre way, Lost Son and Feather Maker were our kids in our past Native American lives. And now it has spilled over into our present life. Sure is sweet to all be reunited.

I have come to believe that the souls that we love and trust the most from our past lives come back in this life to teach us the really hard lessons. During these moments we don't understand what is really happening, but we have chosen them to inject the most difficult pain and profound healing into our life. During the process, we have some immensely unpleasant emotions arise. But underneath it all, we love them.

Of course, I enjoy hanging out and cuddling with Feather Maker, but it's not our destiny to be together for more than a few months. I sense that our age difference is an embarrassment for her. After an unpleasant experience, her ability to trust men is limited. But she is young, free-spirited, and pliable. I let her know she can trust me. After a month, she has a breakthrough. She is more confident and getting bolder around the guys her age that she finds appealing.

But my heart still cries out to be with Swan Song. I am closer to her age. There is something eternally magical about being together. It could last more than a lifetime. Swan Song knows I am affectionately involved with Feather Maker. Feather Maker is aware of my fondness toward Swan Song. It is so obvious. If I make an advance toward Swan Song now, it will be a risky maneuver.

There had been a few tender moments that Swan Song and I shared together, but they did not indicate a genuine romance. Once, I went to visit Swan Song in her tent and stayed until 2:30 a.m. There was a fierce rainstorm outside. I begged her, "Please let me sleep on your floor. Just this one time!" She refused to consider it, and in her serious, deep voice said, "Go home, now!" The coyotes howled in protest as I stepped out of her warm, cozy tent into the blustery rainstorm.

AN UNEXPECTED SURPRISE

Feather Maker and I are still affectionately involved when I visit Swan Song in her tent one lazy morning. Swan Song and I lie down on her bed to talk. And she loves to cuddle. I sure am willing. Yeah, we are a bit impulsive and risqué, but we're just cuddling. It begins to unfold as a stirring, soft, puffy-white-cloud dream. We are in each other's arms. It feels like heaven.

Suddenly, the tent unzips and Feather Maker pops in. There is a deadly silence. We all absorb the impact. The charged emotions of guilt and betrayal come flowing into the tent like burning lava meeting the ocean. Cuddling Swan Song while still involved with Feather Maker was a disastrous mistake. We all feel the consequences. Our hearts are all being ripped apart. Feather Maker looks daggers at me. It's clearly over for Feather Maker and me. The trust I had previously accumulated is now worthless. It vanishes in two seconds flat. She looks emotionally devastated and will never trust me again. She turns and quietly leaves the tent.

The next few moments are awkward. Swan Song and I both feel it. What felt so right a moment ago has disappeared. It has turned to shame. I leave her tent with my head hanging low.

I try to talk with Feather Maker, but it is in vain. It is too late. I lacked the courage to tell Feather Maker that my heart yearned to be with Swan Song. I should have had the guts to initiate closure with her, regardless of the outcome with Swan Song. She is a casualty of my brutal carelessness. I never intended to hurt her. I feel like a lousy shmuck. She deserves to be treated with respect. Instead, I impress another searing-hot brand on her heart. It's a typical one, worn by many women: "TRUST NOT A MAN".

It's a pity that we can't learn lessons about love without getting hurt or inflicting heartbreak. The pain, along with the elated feeling of being in love, lets us know that we are human and fully alive. My heart feels the two extremes: a mix of joy about finally being with Swan Song, and sadness for the way I mistreated Feather Maker.

SWALLOWING POISON

The next day, on the way to her tent, I am anticipating

embracing my beloved Swan Song again. I am having divine thoughts of being in her arms. I unzip the fly of her tent to enter. I peek into the tent. She is lying in bed in all her beauty. Her dirty blond, wavy hair is somewhat messy and unkempt. To me, she is adorable in her silky pajamas. My body is ready to unfold next to hers, but my dearest beloved is not smiling back. I suddenly notice that she is lying in bed next to a hairy, bare-chested man. I find he has a big, detestable smile on his face. It takes me a second to realize that Swan Song is embracing our friend, Lost Son. It's now my turn to swallow the poison. My heart is like a crackle-glass vase that is dropped from a skyscraper. It shatters on the pavement into a zillion pieces.

CRYING OUT

At this point in my life, I am crying out to God for my dream to come true. It's a simple dream. I am not sure why it has become so challenging. I desire to be in a relationship with a decent, spiritual woman. I am ready to place a woman above everything, except God and my health. If I am not healthy, I cannot take care of her and myself, and without God, nothing happens. She is the next-highest priority. This means we place each other above work, money, friends, and even our own extended families, when necessary. I know I am more content when I am in a relationship with a woman. I want to love and cherish a woman as she does me.

I spend most of that winter in Costa Rica actively seeking to find a relationship that I hope will lead to marriage. I have my share of dates with Costa Rican women, but there are lots of cultural differences. Other than my not speaking fluent Spanish, there are big challenges. It has led to some awkward moments. In Costa Rica, one's family is their tribe. If I find a Costa Rican wife, her whole family is welcome to come visit or live in our house whenever they want. I find that difficult to handle.

Before returning for the next season at Omega, I pray to God, "I am ready for a deep, meaningful relationship. Please send me the perfect woman whom I am meant to be with in this life! You know exactly what I need and you know who she is. I am praying that you will bring us together. I am waiting…still waiting…God are you listening?"

CHIEF THUNDER CLOUD

I visit Swan Song a year later. I tell her of my failed attempts at finding a wife in Costa Rica. I let her know I am still searching for the right woman. She listens and then whispers that she has something to tell me. She had not been in a relationship for the past year. With trepidation, I begin to wonder if she is finally about to reveal her affection for me.

She whispers her secret, "I have been dating Chief Thunder Cloud." I can see her excitement; becoming his partner includes an invitation to travel to foreign countries for spiritual-related work within different communities. He is one of our spiritual teachers whom I respect and consider a friend. I admire Chief Thunder Cloud. I consider him a role model. We have friends in the same circles at Omega and in Vermont. For a period, we both went to the same gym, which was my old high school. It's a small world. Over the years, I have given him several Native American token gifts to show him my appreciation. The last one was a cement, three-foot statue of an Indian with a bow and arrow.

Once, I had a strong vision of people from Chief Thunder Cloud's tribe becoming distressed by his actions. I did not know all the people in the vision, but nonetheless the feelings were intense. I felt I must tell him. I sat with him on a stone wall at Omega and shared with him my vision. He was a little alarmed that I knew all this information and confirmed that it had happened. I later learned that my vision had been a huge controversy in his life. Even though Chief Thunder Cloud had moved beyond it, I believe he was concerned about my prophetic insight prying into his past. I believe this vision was revealed to me for a few reasons; it helped me better understand the challenges he faced in his own life and how they led him to where he is today. It also let me know that a man will sometimes make choices that other people detest. These choices can alienate oneself and hurt other's feelings. A man must do what he feels is right. Pride can be a double-edged sword.

He ended our conversation by saying, "If you ever need to talk, consider me like your uncle or grandfather."

Swan Song and I do a ceremony that will bless their being together. If she is happy, then it brings me happiness. Clearly, for whatever reason, she is not comfortable with our being more than friends. I found a red-tailed hawk beside the road; it had been hit by a car. We use the tail feathers to bless their relationship. Swan Song travels and lives part of the season with Chief Thunder Cloud for the next four years.

HANDS ON HEALING

Althea is a meditation teacher at Omega Institute. She shares various techniques for personal spiritual growth through programs designed for the volunteers. She also offers one-on-one treatments. Althea has short, jet-black, wavy hair and grayish eyes. She has features like a Roman goddess and is grounded and firm like a marble statue. She is optimistic, with a large heart for helping others and will tell it like it is with a direct, no-nonsense approach. When Althea offers an invitation or says she will come visit you, she means it. She lives in Sarasota, Florida, but spends occasional weekends during the summer at Omega with her husband and their teenage kids.

One day, during that season, I go to Althea's staff program for volunteers. I am feeling sad and depressed about my past relationships. So far, it has been a disaster to date women in Costa Rica. In addition, I still feel a residue of pain from my marriage that ended fifteen years ago.

During Althea's class, I am given the opportunity to express my feelings surrounding my past relationships. At her suggestion, I lie flat on my back on the floor in the center of the group. They create a circle around me, lying on pillows and blankets, and they place their hands on my body. She instructs the class, "Just be present in your heart. Nobody needs to try to do anything."

God's healing presence arrives. Althea knows how to set the space for healing, when to get out of the way, and how to listen to guidance. If she had a personal agenda for this class, she threw it out the window, because caring for people requires living fully in the present moment.

God's healing spirit begins to work through all those in the room with their hands placed on my body. I start to feel a huge shift. In my vision, I see my fragmented second chakra drop from beneath my body, and a new, brightly-colored one replace it from above. One of the class participants, Terracotta, shifts to hold my head in her hands. After she does this, I visualize brightly-colored gemstones being placed in each of my seven charkas.

I begin letting go of my past relationships. Through the touch of these healers, I feel fully supported. I start to heal on different dimensions. I feel the sadness from my past relationships leave my body. From that moment on, I stop thinking about them, completely. Physically, I feel more solid in my core. Somehow, I am able to let go of the feminine traits I had been nurturing and feel more like a man. I am ready to rip down the silky, golden curtains in my home and go chop some firewood. The group lifts their hands off my body and slides back to form a larger circle again.

After the class is over, I walk out onto the campus at Omega. A friend, G. I. Joe, stops me on the walking path and enthusiastically squeals, "Man, something is different about you! I can't explain it! Something about your whole energy is different!" There has been a huge shift in my essence, and we both know it.

That evening, I go visit Swan Song in her tent. I ask with curiosity, "Do you notice anything different about me?" She lights up and says, "Yes, you are different, you have space for a relationship!" Her statement is welcome confirmation. I never knew why Swan Song was reluctant about our being more than friends. I had pretty much given up on her. I suppose she had her reasons. I never considered I was holding myself back because I had not yet let go of my past relationships. However, it makes sense. I would not hail a taxi if somebody was in it. Why would she want to hail a new relationship if my heart was full with past relationships?

After this day, Swan Song and I spend more and more of our free time together. I am caught off-guard because she suddenly wants to be near me. She begins flirting and inviting me to her tent or she suddenly appears at mine. I get the hint. I was always fond of her, but now there is one big difference. She is allowing me to romantically pursue her, and she likes it.

Chapter 6

Song of Solomon

S ometimes on lazy summer afternoons, Swan Song and I lie together in a hammock by the lake. I especially enjoy napping and waking up next to her. Swan Song enjoys having me read aloud to her. One day, I begin to read Song of Solomon from the Bible. She just lies there with her eyes closed and a soft smile, relishing every word.

> *Beloved*
> *"Let him kiss me with the kisses of his mouth —*
> *for your love is more delightful than wine. Pleasing*
> *is the fragrance of your perfumes; your name is like*
> *perfume poured out. No wonder the young women*
> *love you! Take me away with you — let us hurry!*
> *Let the king bring me into his chambers."*
> *(Song of Songs 1:2-4 NIV)*

After I finish the first chapter, I stop reading. She sighs and says, "You can't stop there! Keep reading it." I say, "Okay," and continue on reading through the next chapter:

> *Beloved*
> *"I am a rose of Sharon, a lily of the valleys."*
> *Lover*
> *"Like a lily among thorns is my darling among*
> *the young women.*
> *Beloved*

"Like an apple tree among the trees of the forest is my beloved among the young men. I delight to sit in his shade, and his fruit is sweet to my taste. Let him lead me to the banquet hall, and let his banner over me be love."

(Song of Songs 2:1-4 NIV)

Whenever I stop, she requests that I keep reading. This happens until it dawns on me that she will not be satisfied unless I read all eight chapters. Eventually, my reading of *Song of Solomon* and other poetry becomes a ritual that we both savor.

A cool summer breeze flows through the scattered trees. Today, Swan Song is sprawled out in a white lawn chair by the lake, receiving a foot massage from Althea. She has unusually small feet that crave to be endlessly caressed. She is relaxing deeply into the bliss — no need to talk to her; she probably will not respond. For her, being touched by another human is a basic necessity, like water or air. She has an uncanny ability to fully receive. She just closes her eyes and takes it all in.

From my perspective, Swan Song emanates love and light to all those around her. She loves being in nature. When given the option, she chooses to curl up in a tent and gaze at a campfire rather than stay in a fancy five-star hotel. She has never owned her own home and lives a nomadic existence, spending time seasonally in tents at Omega and the rest of the season with family, friends, and a few months in the winter living with her partner.

Each season at Omega, her tent is a lush and inviting palace. She has all the modern conveniences, with a hot-pot for tea, a dehumidifier, a large electric heater, and a fridge. One wall holds her hanging closet, with an array of dresses, and underneath it is a large basket filled with cozy, wool sweaters. There is a wooden bookshelf holding a small library of spiritual books, with her lamp and notepad on top. Her queen-size bed has layers of comforters. It is topped off with a star-design quilt and four plush pillows. On the flat headboard is her altar. There she places her candles, photos of spiritual teachers, and various gemstones and trinkets given by friends. The floor is covered with throw-rugs, and her drum and rattles are carefully hanging down in a corner. She jokes about having an entourage of men that come to help her set up and break down her tent, but it actually happens.

She smudges herself daily, usually with sweet-smelling sage from out west. But sometimes she uses sweet grass or palo santo. Years ago she sang in the church choir with her beautiful swan-like voice. She still sings at various gatherings. Women of all ages are drawn to her, and she has a large circle of delightful female companions. She nurtures them with loving hugs of support and provides them with spiritual counsel. Her cheerful disposition and sweet smile draw the attention of both men and women.

I come over and stand above Swan Song. Her dirty-blond, wavy hair is flowing down to her shoulders, and her blue eyes are softly shut. As I begin to softly speak with Althea, she motions for me to kiss Swan Song on her third eye. I hesitate, but it seems like a sweet thing to do, so I gently kiss her forehead. It was more than just a kiss. It was like I had a key and it unlocked the door to our hearts. I believe Althea knew all along that this would happen. I secretly blame her for setting us up to fall madly in love.

From that day forward, we become devoted to each other in an enchanted new way. We secretly enter each other's tents to leave cards, feathers, flowers, and cedar branches on the bed. We smile fondly when we find the gifts upon our return. Our regular gift-giving becomes a way to express how we feel about each other. Care and thought go into the fine details to make it a beautiful arrangement complete with ribbons and wrapping paper. Even the angle in the placement of the gift card is important. The right side needs to be lifted to a 30-degree angle.

Beloved
    "His arms are rods of gold set with chrysolite. His body is like polished ivory decorated with sapphires. His legs are pillars of marble set on bases of pure gold. His appearance is like Lebanon, choice as its cedars. His mouth is sweetness itself; he is altogether lovely."
                                           (Song of Songs 5:14-16 NIV)

Lover
    "How beautiful your sandaled feet, O prince's daughter! Your graceful legs are like jewels, the work of a craftsman's hands. Your navel is a rounded goblet that never lacks blended wine. Your waist is a mound of wheat encircled by lilies."
                                           (Song of Songs 7:1-2 NIV)

At times, we both sense what the other is thinking. Our paths joyously crisscross throughout the day. When I see two red-tailed hawks circling overhead, I anticipate that we will soon be together. Once we are together, it's an eternal picnic of reading poetry, with flirtatious glances to fill in the pauses. We begin to spend most of our free time together in intimate ways. We give each other massages and take walks in the woods, but usually we end up in her tent. Once nobody can see us, our inner desires overflow. We both want to hold each other close. It feels as if a magnetic force is drawing our arms and legs to physically wrap around each other.

Beloved
"His left arm is under my head and his right arm
embraces me. Daughters of Jerusalem, I charge you:
Do not arouse or awake love until it so desires."
(Song of Songs 8:3-4 NIV)

One brisk evening, she is preparing to leave for the weekend. I walk her down to her car. It is under the trees in the parking lot. The stars and moon shine brightly. She wears a big, cuddly sweater. I have on my jeans and a sweat-shirt. Every moment I am with her, I feel life in every cell. Once we are at her car, I give her a gentle hug with both of my arms wrapped around her shoulders. She leans back against her car, and my weight presses firmly against her body. As I look at her, she looks back, and our eyes meet and hold. Then our lips melt together.

After she drives away, I float back up the hill to my tent. I can't stop thinking about her or wipe the soft smile off my face.

A few weeks later, she makes a confession: she says, "I am afraid I am falling in love with you." I smile back at her reassuringly. She says it's the same kind of feeling she had toward the man she married. She never thought she would have that feeling again. I believe that she *really is* afraid to fall in love. Later, I come to understand why.

KEEP IT HIDDEN

Chief Thunder Cloud and Swan Song are still involved in their relationship. She prefers calling him her partner. I am under the impression that she wants to tell "her partner" about our growing affection, but it doesn't happen. Over the next few months, they are together a few times. Each time, I expect she will tell him. But she doesn't do it...she keeps it hidden.

Usually we meet at night in her tent to cuddle. We have conversations about the events of the day. By now, we have spoken about everything under the sun. We have both shared about our past marriages, times at college, our families, and even our pets. She thinks I will get along well with her dad, who is a history buff.

One evening, I am feeling guilty about our being together. I sit up on the edge of her bed and say, "What we are doing does not feel right. We can't keep meeting like this. You need to tell Chief Thunder Cloud." I walk away from her tent in a melancholy mood. I assume she will speak to him, but if she doesn't, I am preparing myself to stay away from her. That's a hard thing for me to even consider. I am falling for her. The spell has been cast.

Beloved
"All night long on my bed I looked for the one my heart loves; I looked for him but did not find him. I will get up now and go about the city, through its streets and squares; I will search for the one my heart loves. So I looked for him but did not find him. The watchmen found me as they made their rounds in the city. "Have you seen the one my heart loves?" Scarcely had I passed them when I found the one my heart loves. I held him and would not let him go till I had brought him to my mother's house, to the room of the one who conceived me."
(Song of Songs 3:1-4 NIV)

She finds me fifteen minutes later, and before I know it, we are dancing under the full moon. She loves to be twirled around. We are both all smiles as she leads me back to her tent. I am hopelessly, helplessly, and happily caught in her web.

*"She threw her arms around him and kissed him,
boldly took his arm and said, "I've got all the mak-
ings for a feast — today I made my offerings, my
vows are all paid, So now I've come to find you,
hoping to catch sight of your face — and here you
are! I've spread fresh, clean sheets on my bed, colorful imported linens. My bed is aromatic with spices and exotic fragrances. Come, let's make love all
night, spend the night in ecstatic lovemaking! My
husband's not home; he's away on business, and he
won't be back for a month."*

(Proverbs 7:13-20 MSG)

Chief Thunder Cloud has a hunch that Swan Song is
seeing another man. He asks her directly on the phone if she
is seeing somebody else. Meanwhile, I am lying on her bed
awaiting her arrival for the evening. She returns and does
her ritual smudging with sage. Cleansing her space or our
bodies with smudging clears away the emotional and psychic energy debris that tends to collect during the day. The
effects of smudging can be surprisingly swift and dramatic.
The rituals can help banish stress, attract love, soothe, and
provide fresh energy.

By now it's engrained; whenever I smell sage I am instantly reminded of her. As usual, she begins to retell the
events that happened during her day. I perk up when she
mentions a phone call from Chief Thunder Cloud. She says,
"He asked me if I was seeing another man." I give a sigh of
relief. Finally, we can be together without any pretension or
a guilty feeling buried in our conscience.

However, she nonchalantly explains, "I told him, 'No!'
It just wasn't right to explain it over the phone." Perhaps in
her mind, she did not think it was lying; just postponing the
truth. I perceive it differently. I am shocked and concerned.

This is serious. If she is willing to lie and justify excuses to her partner, then she will probably treat me the same. I am falling hard for Swan Song. I don't want to believe that she could be this deceptive. I want to believe that at least she is telling *me* the truth. I want to believe I am an exception to her lies. But deep down, I know that her persuasive words and smooth talk have started to taint the truth in ways that sound pleasing to both Chief Thunder Cloud and myself.

> *"Oh what a tangled web we weave, when first we practice to deceive!"*
> — Sir Walter Scott

There is the big fork in the road: I must cautiously make a decision at this junction. I can either abandon the possibility of our having a future relationship, or just keep traveling down this bumpy road. I assume that matters will only get worse if I am involved with a woman who desires to share herself with two men. It is not normal for me to date a woman who is already in a relationship. Yet these un-expected and delightful new circumstances with Swan Song are tossed into my lap in such a light-hearted way that it seems natural.

The journey towards love is passionately exciting, but in the distance a storm is brewing, and the clouds are dark. I begin to contemplate our situation. I know that a woman needs to connect with her partner on a physical, emotional, and spiritual level. Some of her needs, such as feeling secure, are being met by Chief Thunder Cloud. I believe a wom-an will not seek another relationship if her needs are being completely satisfied in her current relationship. She is trying to get her needs met through two different men. I sense that with me, she is craving to fulfil her needs for intimacy, play-fulness, and touch. How long can this go on?

If I twist our scenario enough, I begin to believe it's

ethically acceptable, because they are not married. I convince myself that it's okay to enjoy spending time with Swan Song. Besides, the whole scenario could shift instantly; all she needs to do is tell him about us. I really don't even mind her continuing to work with him. What it is about for me is some quality time when we can be together and sharing our hearts. We feel an insatiable passion for a reason.

It is gradually becoming apparent to me that Swan Song has exhibited a pattern of not leaving her current relationship until she is with a new man. Maybe it needs to happen that way. If that's the case, I recognize that I am willing to play her game.

I pause to consider what was left in the aftermath of her two prior relationships. They were both my friends. It was painful to watch their hearts being torn to shreds. It appeared to me that they were both emotionally traumatized for months.

A few weeks after their break-up, I had heard that My Native Brother had threatened to commit suicide. At one point, Swan Song believed his plan may have been to also hurt her. She was so fearful that she took refuge in a friend's trailer. She thought he had a gun. She hoped he wouldn't be able to find her there. It seemed to her that he was angry about losing her and didn't give a damn about what happened.

She confided that being in a temporary relationship with Lost Son was an easy way to break it off with My Native Brother. She said, "I told him up front: the reason I am with you is to end my last relationship." She said his response was to say, "Don't tell me that; I do not want to hear that." When I later shared this version with Lost Son, he said, "It is an off-based statement. What she had told me up front was that she was essentially on the rebound from the relationship with My Native Brother. She introduced this other perspective a few months after we had become intimate. I was pretty much emotionally involved and committed to a significant degree by that time. It was definitely not what I would consider up front."

LOST SON'S BREAK-UP (OR BREAKDOWN)

Late one afternoon, I stopped by to visit Swan Song after she had dissolved her relationship with Lost Son. Her disrespectful treatment had left him feeling like an expendable pawn. He was not taking it lightly. Swan Song was in her tent. Lost Son had stationed himself on a folding easy chair thirty feet away under a tree. He was badgering her through the walls of her tent with beer-enhanced slurs about their breakup. When I arrived at her tent, she was attempting to drown him out by playing music. She had a look of despair. I learned that his slanderous remarks, speckled with colorful obscenities, had been going on for a few hours. I felt compassion for Swan Song and Lost Son. Her chosen method to defuse the drama with My Native Brother by involving Lost Son had worked out to some degree, but in the process she had ruthlessly hurt Lost Son's feelings. His pain was erupting in spurts of anger.

After being disregarded, Lost Son attempted to drown his sorrow. After finishing his seventh beer, he was in a defiant, ass-kicking mood. As a friend, I felt I could resolve the situation by talking with him. Swan Song looked afraid. She was asking me for protection. I had never seen Lost Son this disheveled. I stepped out of her tent and began to walk toward him. He kicked a lawn chair in my direction. In my attempt to avoid it, I stumbled and bruised my shin on an iron tent stake. Before I could get next to him, he let loose a series of rapid-fire accusations about my involvement with Swan Song (all accentuated with vulgar profanities). My adrenalin began to rise. He was rude and out of control. I couldn't reason with him. He was inflamed and tumultuous. Definitely not the right moment for consoling. I was slightly afraid of what would happen next. I didn't want to provoke him. I turned and went back into her tent.

Swan Song and I discussed our options. We decided it was best to call upon Omega security. Two big men arrived in a golf cart. They took control and quickly persuaded Lost Son that it was in his best interest to leave the vicinity.

WARRANTED DANGER

How could a woman stir up such a violent reaction from two decent men? These guys are my friends whom I respect. Perhaps, there is warranted danger accompanied with mild deception. I will proceed with caution. Of course, I will not be emotionally incapacitated or deceived by her. I am solid and immune to this type of fate. At least, I am naive enough to believe that. In the end, it will all be worthwhile, once Swan Song and I are together.

> "Say to wisdom, "You are my sister," and call understanding your intimate friend; that they may keep you from an adulteress, from the foreigner who flatters with her words. For at the window of my house I looked out through my lattice, and I saw among the naive, and discerned among the youths a young man lacking sense, passing through the street near her corner; and he takes the way to her house, in the twilight, in the evening, in the middle of the night and in the darkness. And behold, a woman comes to meet him, dressed as a harlot and cunning of heart. She is boisterous and rebellious, her feet do not remain at home; she is now in the streets, now in the squares, and lurks by every corner."
>
> (Proverbs 7:4-12 NASB)

CONCERNED

I must admit, I feel slightly uneasy when I look deeply into Swan Song's eyes. Sometimes they are cloudy and silted. Eyes are meant to be the gateway to the soul. When I gaze into her eyes, I do not feel she is fully able to trust me. But I will extend to her my trust. She needs to know that she can trust me. To my knowledge, I have never done anything to mislead or betray her, but maybe another man has. It doesn't feel like these issues revolving around trust are her natural state. I believe something traumatic happened.

Two thoughts continue to gnaw away. First of all, if Swan Song is not faithful and honest to Chief Thunder Cloud, why would she treat me any differently? Secondly, if being together and not telling him is deceptive, then it is not just on her part, but mine as well. This is compounded because Chief Thunder Cloud is my friend, too. This situation has the potential to get really nasty. It could even become explosive.

But alas, my heart sings a completely different song. The melody is sweet and her skin is soft whenever I am with her. Our lips drip with honey, and she is as smooth as oil. She has expressed that no harm exists in our being together. By now, the fragrance of love overrules anything that subtly resembles common sense.

Lover
"How beautiful you are, my darling! Oh, how beautiful! Your eyes behind your veil are doves. Your hair is like a flock of goats descending from the hills of Gilead. You are altogether beautiful, my darling; there is no flaw in you. You have stolen my heart, my sister, my bride; you have stolen my heart with one glance of your eyes, with one jewel

of your necklace."

(Song of Songs 4:1,7,9 NIV)

On the few occasions when Chief Thunder Cloud comes to visit Omega, I am shuffled under the rug by Swan Song until he leaves. During these times, I find myself emotionally tormented. Once, the three of us ended up in the same room during ecstatic chant. It was worse than medieval torture. This woman, whom I consider my beloved, was being hugged and affectionately touched on her back by another man, in front of my very eyes. Inside, I was emotionally in shambles. It was like a burning hot rod was just shoved inside my heart. I wanted to shout out and cry in agony. Instead, I consoled myself with lies. I whispered to myself, *she is only pretending to want to be with him; she really loves me.*

Yet, I feel compassion for Chief Thunder Cloud. He is left in the dark. He will obviously be hurt if (or should I say when) he discovers we are lovers. It's awkward because I have no reason to conceal my love for her, not even from him, but she insists that everything must be kept hidden. I begin to feel shame in public. I am given no option; I must withhold showing affection toward the woman I love. Even our friends must not know.

Friends
"Who is this coming up from the wilderness leaning on her beloved?"
Beloved
"Under the apple tree I roused you; there your mother conceived you, there she who was in labor gave you birth. Place me like a seal over your heart, like a seal on your arm; for love is as strong as death, its jealousy unyielding as the grave. It burns like

blazing fire, like a mighty flame. Many waters cannot quench love; rivers cannot sweep it away. If one were to give all the wealth of one's house for love, it would be utterly scorned."

(Song of Songs 8:5-7 NIV)

When others are near, it's inappropriate to give her long hugs or to send those loving glances. Instead, we whisper in the shadows of the night, behind-the-scene. Occasionally, I hold Swan Song and she cries. There is a lot going on inside both of us. I consider telling Chief Thunder Cloud myself, just to break it all wide open. Once, I sit down by the riverside to pray with my chanupa before I write him a letter that carefully explains our romantic involvement, but Swan Song pleads, "Don't send it!" Now, if I go against her wishes, I feel like I am betraying her, too. I know that eventually Chief Thunder Cloud will find out. I figure it's best to wait until she finds the courage to tell him herself.

Chapter 7

Available and Unattached

At the end of that season, I invite Swan Song to visit me in Costa Rica with one condition: she is *not* in a relationship with Chief Thunder Cloud.

She says, "I will not buy a plane ticket unless I am available and unattached."

I make my stand and don't look back. I feel good about myself. I am singing a new song filled with painful honesty, patience, and integrity.

I do a ceremony in Costa Rica to let myself know when Swan Song is ready to visit. On a pencil-thin tree branch on the far side of a brook, I tie a red piece of fabric. I request that when Swan Song and Chief Thunder Cloud both have clarity about her being, as she calls it, "available and un-attached", the red fabric will fall down and float away in the brook. I learned from the experience with My Native Brother that it's not spiritually ethical to influence another's actions or thoughts in a relationship. This time, I will wait patiently.

Swan Song and I first speak seriously about her visiting in January. She is not yet "available and unattached." The red fabric still hangs over the brook. I look over and check it as we head into February. A heavy rainstorm washes away the log bridge that allowed me to easily cross over the brook. I can't see how well it is hanging on. Swan Song tells me she is close to having the conversation with Chief Thunder Cloud. I feel empathy for the unwelcome news he will receive. I decide to go over and check on the red fabric up close. Maybe I can sage it and he will receive some sort of comfort.

While having this thought, I take one step down the embankment, and my foot flies sky-high. I am thrown down hard in the mud as if slam-dunked flat on my back. The wind is knocked out of my lungs. I gasp for breath. My first thought is of the spirit of Chief Thunder Cloud. He must have kicked me in the ass. It comes with the spiritual reminder: as a man, he does not need nor desire any comfort from me. I stand up covered in mud. I can hear his spirit laughing. I also begin to laugh out loud. He got me good that time!

While in Costa Rica, I buy a female Rhodesian Ridgeback dog named Thunder. During my early morning walks with her, I watch a lone hawk. Near the end of February, it has found a mate. The two are together. I know it's a sign that Swan Song and I will soon be together. There is a great spot to swim in the river behind the home I am renting. It's set amongst the rainforest with slabs of gray clay layered in the side bank. While swimming, I sense the presence of Swan Song's spirit in the water. She does love the water. Time is a thin veil, like a weathered leaf, with no past or present. Her spirit has arrived slightly before her body. I can sense her swimming nearby in the water. I write down all these prophetic signs as a poem. I send it to Swan Song prior to her arrival.

Lying under the Buffalo Robe

When a red-tailed hawk soars above me,
I know your spirit is on the way.
From the heart of the universe we heal and pray.
Lying under a pine tree,

I feel the earth.

When two red-tailed hawks soar in a circle,
I know our spirits are together.
From the heart of the universe, our love is born.
Lying under the buffalo robe,
we share our love.

When the red-tailed hawks migrate by the hundreds,
I know our spirits have united.
From the heart of the universe, our dreams come to life.
Lying under the stars,
we give thanks.

Hurray! Hurray! Swan Song tells me she has purchased a ticket for three and a half weeks in Costa Rica starting in March.

She says, "I am now available and unattached."

This is a powerful step that she has taken of her own free will. I am overwhelmed. She is consciously and deliberately making a decision to leave Chief Thunder Cloud to be with me.

Lover

"My dove in the cleft of the rock, in the hiding places on the mountain side, show me your face, let me hear your voice; for your voice is sweet, and your face is lovely. Catch for us the foxes, the little foxes that ruin the vineyards, our vineyards that are in bloom."

Beloved

"My lover is mine and I am his; he browses among the lilies. Until the day breaks and the shadows flee, turn, my lover, and be like the gazelle or like

a young stag on the rugged hills."

(Song of Songs 2:14-17 NIV)

She does not tell me any of the details about her final conversation with Chief Thunder Cloud, but her whole choice of words (or lack of words) seems a bit out of character. She ended a major relationship with one of our friends and does not want to share the details of how it went? That's not like her. Maybe it is deeply personal. I'm sure it was not easy. Given the situation, I am not going to pry. I am thankful she honored my request. What is more important is that she and I have new-born integrity. Her decision will have a huge impact on the lives of all three of us.

I am filled with joy as I anticipate our time together. My current role is as a facilitator in the Cristo Morpho Volunteer Program. I explain to the volunteers that I want to take a week to be with Swan Song. We desire to travel to Bocas del Toro in Panama to celebrate her birthday. We discuss the situation. I express how important it is for me to have this time with Swan Song, but I don't want to falter in my commitment. The volunteers boost the ante. They desire the full month of March to explore Costa Rica. They want to take that time to travel to the Envision Festival, explore the Pacific Coast, travel with friends, and visit other spiritual communities.

SWAN SONG ARRIVES IN COSTA RICA

I am standing outside the airport among a crowd of dark-skinned Latinos and overzealous taxi drivers, when Swan Song walks out from the glass doorway. I have a soft smile as I watch her emerge from the crowd. She has a big sun hat and wears a bright, flowered, knee-length dress. Swan Song travels with more baggage than most women, but in her case I welcome it all. She looks around trying to find her bearings amongst the crowd. I am standing silently fifteen feet away, admiring her. She starts to walk in my direction, but has not yet noticed me. When she is a few feet in front of me, she begins to teeter back and forth awkwardly, as one does to avoid bumping into a stranger. Suddenly she recognizes me. She catches herself in midair, smiles, and transforms her stumble into a fling, landing in my open arms. Our adventure has begun!

On the bus, she stares out the open window, mesmerized by the rainforest as we wind up paved roads through the steep mountains of Braulio Carrillo National Park. It rains regularly in these high mountain passes. Waterfalls spill out from high, canyon-size walls carpeted with large green tropical leaves that shimmer in the misty fresh air.

One month earlier, I went to a roadside gift shop and bargained with a short Latino woman to purchase a batik-style, orange and black-striped hammock made to hold three people. This hammock is reserved for Swan Song and me. I kept it hidden away from the volunteers until her arrival. I place two hammock hooks between coconut trees on the far bank overlooking the river. The cool, steady breeze makes it an ideal place. Here we shall cuddle, take lazy naps, read books, and share our hearts.

Beloved
"Come, my lover, let us go to the countryside, let us spend the night in the villages. Let us go early to the vineyards to see if the vines have budded, if the blossoms have opened, and if the pomegranates are in bloom — there I will give you my love."
(Song of Songs 7:11-12 NIV)
Lover
"I have come into my garden, my sister, my bride; I have gathered my myrrh and my spice. I have eaten

*my honeycomb and my honey; I have drunk my wine
and my milk."*
Friends say
   *"Eat, O friends, and drink; drink your fill of lov-
er."*

(Song of Songs 5:1 NIV)

Upon her arrival, we prepare to recline in the king-size, batik hammock. Swan Song has her own way of doing things. Sometimes it's better, but it is different from how I would normally do it. She explains, "The most comfortable way to sit in a hammock is diagonal with your head on one end and mine on the other." I admit it is pretty comfortable. Plus, I get her cute bare feet to play with.

Another way Swan Song and I are different is the rate that we make decisions and act upon them. It will take her a month to make a major decision and another few weeks to act, whereas it will take me an hour to decide and it will be done later that day. Symbolically, she is a turtle and I am a rabbit.

Sometimes when I am waiting for her, I often think, but seldom say, "What is taking you so long?" At other times, she will look absolutely puzzled and exclaim, "You made that decision and did it already!"

When we come together as a team to make decisions, it's a learning process: I slow down and she speeds up. It's all part of the universal plan to find harmony between a man and a woman. Together, we teach each other to respect our differences.

Today Swan Song and I are sitting crossed-legged in the hammock facing each other. This way we can be fully present and gaze into each other's eyes. This is our first deep conversation. She starts by saying, "You need to listen and understand: I am here as a friend. I am here to be free. I don't want to place any limits on us."

I do listen, but in my book, we have been more than friends already. We have been sleeping next to each other for months. I understand she needs some space and perhaps to take a step back before we can take a step forward. As a woman, she is unpredictable. I gave up trying to figure out or anticipate what she wants or will do next. All I can do is enjoy being with her.

I prepared the women's volunteer room for her to stay in during her visit. After the first night, she drags her bags into my room. She wants to sleep next to me on my full-size bed. It's a peculiar friendship she desires. At first, I instinctively hesitate to let her sleep with me. Of course, we both want to cuddle up, and that is nothing new, but I am concerned about the moments when my passion and hers start to rise.

LET'S TALK ABOUT SEX

Prior to now, she has never been available and unattached. If she wants to sleep together now, we better talk about sex. I request that if we are to have sex for the first time, we discuss it and both comply. As a safety net, I suggest we wait 24-hours after we both agree. This way we won't slip and go there during the height of passion. She doesn't understand why there needs to be a 24-hour window.

I recall a conversation we had about sex in her tent while cuddling in her bed at Omega. It shocked me when she said, "I will not marry a man unless we first have sex." I stare at her, wide-eyed, "Are you serious?" She replies, "What if the sex is lousy?" That set me back. I tell her, "It is my intention to wait for sex until after I am married." I did not always have this belief. In my past I had sex before marriage and after my marriage ended.

Let's discuss this issue. It is an important one, especially for young adults. Some believe it's biblical to wait until marriage before sex. The Bible does not use the phrase "premarital sex." But what the Bible does talk about is sexual immorality.

> *"Flee from sexual immorality. All other sins a person commits are outside the body, but whoever sins sexually, sins against their own body."*
>
> (1 Corinthians 6:18 NIV)

"Sexual immorality" is the English translation of the Greek word porneia, which means "fornication." Fornication means "voluntary sexual intercourse between two unmarried persons."

Following the Bible is an excellent reason, but I have other reasons. I want to get to know the woman and love her as my best friend before we get married. I desire a mutual commitment for better or worse, regardless of our sex being great or lousy. I also feel that waiting somehow sanctifies the marriage. There is a purity exhibited, even if they both had prior sex. It shows discipline. Their actions honor sex as sacred, both before and after the marriage. Lastly, I want to feel self-respect and respect for my partner and her beliefs. Sex is important, but love and respect go hand-in-hand as the foundation for a sound marriage.

Swan Song, having been raised in a Christian home, has shared that she used to believe in marriage before sex. But she was not able to keep her quintessential values. She eventually gave in to peer pressure. She went to parties and was part of the popular crowd. She sadly confesses, "I had sex before marriage. After that I felt soiled." I feel empathetic. She continues, "After I did it once, there was no reason to not have sex with other men."

Chapter 8

Swan Song in Costa Rica

Together, we create our own little tropical paradise. She often reads or takes a lazy afternoon nap in the hammock. As I live with Swan Song, I begin to learn her ways, but she still whips out surprises. At first, all she wants to eat is fruit. I make rice, chicken, and vegetables for dinner and all she wants is watermelon. Her diet consists of watermelon, pineapples, melons, papaya, and mangos for the first five days. I begin to wonder if I am living with a woman or an orangutan. She proclaims, "The fruit here is fresh and yummy!"

Friends
   "Where has your beloved gone, most beautiful of women? Which way did your beloved turn, that we may look for him with you?"
Lover
   "My beloved has gone down to his garden, to the beds of spices, to browse in the gardens and to gather lilies. I am my beloved's and my beloved is mine; he browses among the lilies."

(Song of Songs 6:1-3 NIV)

Beloved
   "Your plants are an orchard of pomegranates with choice fruits, with henna and nard, nard and saffron, calamus and cinnamon, with every kind of incense tree, with myrrh and aloes and all the finest

spices. You are a garden fountain, a well of flowing
water streaming down from Lebanon.
Lover
"Awake, north wind, and come, south wind!
Blow on my garden, that its fragrance may spread
everywhere. Let my beloved come into his garden
and taste its choice fruits."

(Song of Songs 4:13-16 NIV)

Eventually, she starts to eat warm food and salads. We take turns making meals. When she makes a salad, both hands dive into the bowl to mix it up, which I find rather cute. I don't know how I have survived all these years without squeezing lemons and pouring large quantities of salt on all my meals. It must have been mandatory in her home.

I am surprised to find out that she likes to play board games. We enjoy playing chess, and for being fairly new at it, she is better than I expected. Each chess game is a ritual battle of teasing. I let her grab a piece or two of mine before we begin, just to make it fair. I come prepared with hot tea and coconut chunks to dip in peanut butter. She has popcorn and half a bar of chocolate for when the battle gets tough.

Before we start, I smile and ask, "Are you ready to lose... again?" She will respond by ruthlessly kicking my butt and playfully say, "I won again."

CAHUITA NATIONAL PARK

In this area, the rainforest comes down to meet the beach. Nearby, there is Cahuita National Park and the Gandoca Manzanillo Reserve. We hike through Cahuita National Park, which follows the Caribbean coastline for a seven km trail. It holds the claim as the largest living coral reef in Costa Rica, with 35 species of coral and over 400 different types of fish. In the early morning, on occasion, I have seen dolphins leaping up as they travel down the coast. This park has abundant wildlife, and as a photographer, I am excited to take close-up photos of howler and white-faced monkeys, iguanas, the yellow viper, and the slow-moving three-toed sloth.

There had been a big storm which scattered coral and shells along the beach. I have a surreal sense that I need to find the perfect conch shell. I keep searching, but find only broken ones. I am caught up in fondling all the shells, like a five-year-old child. I gather a collection of shells in a sack. Swan Song chooses a few shells with exceptional beauty. I excuse myself to go behind a tree with some toilet paper. As I squat down and peer under my butt, there it is…the perfect conch shell. It's smooth, bleach-white, and artistically designed with rose-pink swirls and curves on the inner caverns. It's the one I came to find!

DON CANDIDO MORALES, INDIGENOUS PLANT MEDICINE

One of my indigenous friends is Don Candido Morales. He operates an indigenous cultural center called Tururuwak in the small village of Patino. He offers indigenous plant medicine treatments and has knowledge of 1,500 plants. He learned about the rainforest plant medicine from his mother, and it has been passed down through the generations for over 5,000 years.

Swan Song and I visit Don Candido. He utilizes various methods to diagnose a patient, but he often starts by pressing points on their feet. The areas that are sensitive indicate a specific system or organs that need attention. They are his top priorities. He was a savior by removing copper from my liver, and gave me a rainforest remedy for dengue fever that brought my blood count back to normal in two days. It left all the doctors baffled.

Swan Song receives a diagnosis and treatment with rainforest plant medicine. He keeps calling Swan Song my wife, as does Maria at the internet café. I quietly smile about it and don't bother correcting them anymore. When we are together, we anticipate each other's actions. We find ways to provide each other with simple pleasures. Our rituals for greeting and saying goodbye are filled with hugs and soft glances of affection. Once a friend couldn't understand why I was so crazy about her, until he saw a picture of Swan Song and me. Then he understood; we were meant to be together.

Don Candido invites us to come over in the evening to join him and his sons in a fire ceremony designed for friends. Fresh fruit is offered at his gatherings as a way to make sure everybody has a sweet disposition. He makes a fire using pago wood on a square, indoor, stone fire hearth. We stand at the sides to represent each of the four directions. In their tradition, they honor the north as the eagle, the east as the dolphin, the south as the jaguar, and the west as the bear. We circle around the fire to each get a chance to represent all four directions.

Don Candido places dried plants on the flames. When Swan Song is standing in the south, the smoke wafts around her. He speaks in Spanish, and his son, Enrique, translates: "The smoke goes in the direction of the person who is in need of that type of energy or healing."

BIRTHDAY MONTH

Swan Song makes a big deal of birthdays. She calls March her birthday month, and it grants her special attention for 31 days. For her actual birthday, we visit Bocas del Toro in Panama for five days. There are a few areas where one can commonly spot dolphins. Swan Song has swum with dolphins before, and they allowed her to touch them. It was a moving experience. It's my hope that she can get close to them on her birthday.

Unfortunately, we don't spot any dolphins. However, in the middle of a downpour, we seek shelter at the fancy Dolphin Hotel.

For her birthday treat, she buys chips and a beer to consume while we play our ritual chess game on the balcony overlooking the sea. We depart the next day for a daylong boat tour. We snorkel in the turquoise Caribbean Ocean near gigantic, orange sponge coral with starfish the size of hubcaps, black eels, and an underwater parade of angel and parrotfish.

It feels great after swimming to lie on the beach completely wet and bake in the hot sun next to Swan Song. And we take long walks holding hands on the stunningly beautiful, wide, sandy beaches. Whenever we are together, there is a divine spark in our eyes. Finding each other is a gift. I am grateful for every moment we are together. In reality, we never know how long it will last.

I have engrained precious memories of being on the beach in Maine during a vacation with my past wife, Forevermore. During a memorable walk on the beach, I had taken a photo of our names drawn in the sand, encompassed within a heart symbol. I cherished it and had a photograph enlarged for our wedding guests to sign with a glitter pen.

Now, while being on the beach, memories of Forevermore and Swan Song are beginning to merge. A similar, strong feeling of love is surfacing. As we stop to sit on the beach, I confess to Swan Song that I am feeling love for her, as if she were my wife. I turn to her and say, "I never thought I would feel this kind of love for a woman again." She quietly responds, "I understand. It's okay to have those feelings. Other guys have felt that way about me."

We make it a complete birthday vacation by dining out overlooking the ocean. We fill our evenings by playing pool and ping-pong on the hostel veranda. She plays a viciously fun game of ping-pong, but her pool skills are pathetic. The next day, she insists on paying for both of us to go on the zip line adventure. It is under the guise that it's her birthday week. We each strap on a harness and glide over a series of cables from one rainforest treetop to another.

THE CHOCOLATE MASSAGE

On our return, I stop to pick up paint for my three-bedroom home in Buena Vista. The volunteers will soon be returning, and it will be our project to paint the house. I pick up a five-gallon bucket of cream-colored paint because it costs a lot less in Panama than in Costa Rica. But I must carry it a quarter mile across the bridge that connects the two countries.

We return for her last week at the rental house. We are feeling relaxed as one does during a lazy beach vacation. Prior to her arrival, I had a few dreams about making love with Swan Song. They felt prophetic, which is much different than a fantasy. A prophetic dream has great significance. I am sent this message for a reason. I know that we will make love. Remember Swan Song gave me one of her prerequisites for being married: she must have sex first. One doesn't casually toss this kind of information out to anybody. I contemplate it.

At this point in my life, if I marry someone, I want it to be her. I truly believe that if we don't have sex, I can't even be considered a potential marriage partner. We have had an intimate friendship for several years. We have gotten to know each other. We love and respect each other. Now that she is available and unattached, it seems natural that sex will soon be on the table. (no pun intended) Of course, I would enjoy making love to her, but it means I will compromise my values regarding sex only after marriage. It causes some inner conflict. I can't keep my standard and meet her prerequisite.

One evening while lying in bed, we revisit the discussion about having sex. We both give consent. I would be a liar if I said the only reason I wanted sex was to meet her prerequisite. The first time we make love we are impulsive and the 24-hour window is disregarded. Making love is always a sacred act. I am not going to describe our lovemaking scenes. What I will share is that we treat each other with tenderness, and with her, I am always in my heart.

The next day, we take turns giving each other massages. She bought some chocolate designed for massage. We are playing around and having some fun with it. As I lick some chocolate off her shoulder, I think I have figured out what she meant by saying, "being free without placing any limits."

NO VISIT TO BUENA VISTA

Even though Swan Song badly wants to visit my land in Buena Vista, I get strong guidance that we should not go there. I know there must be a good reason why. I have always been guided with precision about if and when people should come visit my land in Buena Vista. I often share with volunteers the exact day I feel they are guided to arrive and I usually know the day they will depart. There are poisonous snakes, spiders, and scorpions, but in ten years nobody has been bothered by them. I feel God's protection while we are on our land, but I must obey His given guidance.

"I have given you authority to trample on snakes and scorpions and to overcome all the power of the enemy; nothing will harm you." (Luke 10:19 NIV)

However, she continually persists. She exclaims, "I came all this way expecting to see your land!" Tomorrow is the last full day before she starts her journey to leave Costa Rica. Finally, I give in. I reluctantly reply, "Okay, we can go visit my land in Buena Vista tomorrow."

In the morning, we sit down on the back porch to discuss the plans. As we start talking, it becomes apparent to me that I am going against God's desire for the sake of pleasing the woman I love. I feel strongly that I can't allow this to happen. In her presence, I break down and cry out with tears, "Please God, forgive me for whatever will happen! I know that we are acting against your will."

Swan Song finds compassion for me. I am relieved to know she is willing to compromise when she sees how upset I am. We settle instead for a day on the beach in Cahuita. We have a picnic lunch. There is a steady breeze as we hold each other close, lying in the sand. We throw her sarong over our heads to close out the world. We share our deepest thoughts in whispers. I can still smell the sea and her warm, sandy skin next to mine. Our time together has come to an end. The next day, I escort her on the bus back to the airport.

The volunteers and I live the next few weeks in Buena Vista. We plant another phase of fruit trees: one that includes mangosteen, jack fruit, guanabana, and some edible greens like pacific spinach. As a group project, we paint the house inside and out. Afterwards, we take time to explore a part of our rainforest land. We start by following a brook; along the way, we observe red and green poison dart frogs and wild yellow plums. Hundreds of them have dropped into the brook and gathered bobbing in a pool.

When I find time to send Swan Song a few emails, I write enthusiastically about how I can't wait to be together again. Our time together had a natural flow that was easy-going and filled with delightful moments. Our relationship reached a whole new level of intimacy. I tell her I am excited that our relationship is deepening. I think to myself...*Finally, the two of us can be together in public. There will be no more façade. The wall she built to keep our love affair concealed from her partner can now be dismantled.*

A week later, she responds with an email that resounds in my mind like an echo shouted out from the top of the Grand Canyon.

"I am Not...not...not available
for a Relationship...relationship...relationship.
How does this make you Feel...feel...feel?"

Chapter 9

Sacrum Meltdown

I return to Vermont in May after the Cristo Morpho Volunteer Program ends. I have a grueling trip back with heavy luggage. I ride a Mountain bike with a backpack down the mountain and then 24 kilometers into town to catch the bus. Then I end up sleeping on the floor in the airport terminal during my layover in Austin, Texas.

Upon my return, I attempt to email and call Swan Song, but there is no response. I am floundering in disbelief after I learn that Swan Song left for Europe with Chief Thunder Cloud. In the last email I had received, she vaguely explained, "I will not be available to communicate with you while I am away." Swan Song is obviously no longer "available or unattached." I have been deceived.

She had asked, "How do I feel?" I am thoroughly confused! The rough return trip put some strain on my back, and I am struck with a feeling of being emotionally abandoned. I experience what I call a full-blown sacrum meltdown. Basically, my core muscles lose control and forget how to function. I am in shock. My sacrum has gone numb. It is unable or unwilling to feel nor comprehend what Swan Song has done. And it's not alone; my heart and mind are equally lost.

Chief Thunder Cloud is a man of integrity. I can't say I have always been that way. But now I am upholding integrity to the best of my ability. From my perspective, I made my stand for integrity and Swan Song used it as a platform for her deception.

For the next thirty days, I place my full effort into re-educating my core muscles so they know how to function. I go to physical therapy, massage, Pilates, and chiropractic treatments. This regimen slowly strengthens my core muscles. Eventually, I regain most of my normal physical muscle functions. I feel like I am recovering from a near-fatal car accident. When I tell people my condition was caused by a relationship, they raise their eyebrows.

I get no response from Swan Song for the next month. I am coming undone and start to lose it. I conjure up all sorts of horrid conclusions about her, none of which include me in the scenario. In a moment of desperation, I call Lost Son and share my dilemma. I feel better after talking to him. We have both been gravely wounded by Swan Song, and he can relate to my suffering.

I force myself to start doing serious meditation as a way to control the torrents of *self*-destructive thoughts. It's like my mind is being attacked by Japanese kamikaze pilots. Their target is my self-worth, my self-esteem, and my self-respect. Finally, a month later, Swan Song returns from Europe. Upon her return, we speak on the phone. I am comforted by her voice and my sacrum rapidly recovers another few fractions. We need to meet face-to-face for a heart-to-heart conversation.

DEVIL'S ROCK

We meet twice in Vermont. Our first encounter is at Lake Willoughby. Being at this lake with its deep, cold waters is comfortably significant. It is a sunny afternoon. I bring bikes and we ride them along the paved road following the shoreline until we come to Devil's Rock. This is where young men, like myself and friends, would test our bravery by plunging thirty feet off the rock cliff into icy cold water.

Swan Song and I sit on Devil's Rock watching the wind push the waves from the north shore as we soak in the sun. We both know that we desperately need to talk about what transpired, carefully. We sit still in silence for several minutes to get in touch with our feelings. We both need to find the right words. Swan Song is oblivious to how much I have suffered. I am feeling vulnerable. I gave her my heart and soul in Costa Rica.

I delicately explain how I felt frustrated about not being able to communicate with her for a month and about my sacrum meltdown. It had been overwhelming. I continue to tell her all the challenges I am facing during my recovery. She admits that not communicating for a month was not a good idea. She apologizes. It caused problems for herself and others. Omega Institute had also attempted to contact her regarding her work schedule and was unable to reach her. It almost placed her job in jeopardy.

While she is talking, I unravel that Swan Song *never* told Chief Thunder Cloud that she was going to spend time with *me* in Costa Rica. She says she told him she was going to Costa Rica for a vacation. It was a far cry from ending her relationship with him. She returned directly from Costa Rica to live in his home, and then they travelled to Europe together. It is obvious they are still partners. We do not even discuss her deception. It is somehow deflected and diffused. I can't yet comprehend it. My emotions have frozen. They are not willing to accept that she lied to me. It might mean I would forfeit what I cherish more than life…her.

Upon their return from Europe, he insisted firmly that she tell him whom she had spent time with in Costa Rica. It was then she finally broke down and told him. She gave him my name. She suggested that I avoid any form of contact with him in the future. She says, "Just stay away from him." My sense from what she says is that he is fuming with indignation toward me for my actions, while Swan Song is above reproach. I wonder if Chief Thunder Cloud knows how badly we have *both* been deceived.

She has mastered the art of not revealing pertinent information. Trust is the foundation for an intimate relationship. Trust means full disclosure. Little things like where she is going next and with whom are pretty damn relevant to him and to me. With carefully chosen words, she skirts the real issues. I had assumed by misleading hints in our conversations that she was going to stay with her parents after leaving Costa Rica. She never came out and said it, but it was implied. All along, she had the intention of returning to Chief Thunder Cloud.

CHEWING GUM NUMB

I was not angry when the deception first occurred. Actually, I felt some relief in knowing that Chief Thunder Cloud had finally coaxed the truth out of her. Afterwards, my whole world began to crumble. Not just because she deceived me — it is true, what she did was inconceivable to my mind and heart. She built up my trust and self-esteem. I thought she was standing by my side. I was trying to live with honor. She took it all away. She destroyed that beautiful piece of artwork called integrity. She took an ice pick and began marring it. Then she handed it back, worthless.

It took me a few more years before I could process it all and get in touch with my real feelings. Around that time, I have a conversation with a woman from the prior community where Swan Song lived for several years before Omega. Our topic is deception in relationships. Out of the blue, she describes a pretty woman, with wavy blond hair and blue eyes, who left their community to go to Omega. She said, "This woman deceived and hurt a lot of men. She would use her beauty and charm to get away with it." I perked up. She may not have known it, but she was referring to Swan Song.

Only then did I realize that Swan Song has been deceiving men for decades. It seems that deception became her standard method of operating with men. I feel empathy for her situation. I love her regardless. She might even be doing it all subconsciously. I don't think she is aware of how deceptive she is with men or how much her lies batter a man's soul.

"With persuasive words she led him astray; she seduced him with her smooth talk. All at once he followed her like an ox going to the slaughter, like a deer stepping into a noose till an arrow pierces his liver, like a bird darting into a snare, little knowing it will cost him his life. Now then, my sons, listen to me; pay attention to what I say. Do not let your heart turn to her ways or stray into her paths. Many are the victims she has brought down; her slain are a mighty throng. Her house is a highway to the grave, leading down to the chambers of death."

(Proverbs 7:21-27 NIV)

CARING FOR THE HEART

We all have our issues. I am in no way an exception. But one's mate can witness their partner's issues more clearly than they can. Swan Song is great at pointing out mine: I change my plans, make fast decisions, and sometimes I am judgmental. Sometimes it's damn annoying, but overall I am grateful to know. I truly hope, more than I can express, that Swan Song can find healing for her deeper issues. I know I can't change her or heal her. I love her and accept her as she is. But I want her to be a woman of integrity, even if she is not my partner. I want what is best for her. I will eternally support her in this way.

While in Vermont, I make an appointment with a couple who are the New England Caring for the Heart counselors. I hope that Swan Song and I can attend some joint sessions. The appointment happens by fate to fall on one of the only other days that we could be together. Swan Song agrees to accompany me to a preliminary conversation with the counselors.

A week after our rendezvous at Devil's Rock, we meet with the counselors. Their advice is that Swan Song should, as the first step, receive individual counseling for her deeper issues. I am surprised when Swan Song agrees to come back for three days of counseling later in the fall. I have faith in this form of Christ-based counseling. I know it's possible for Jesus to heal her past traumas, including whatever happened in her first marriage. I have experienced it. I am excited for her. She is willing to work on her own stuff. It's a vital component of any conscious relationship. I await her counseling sessions enthusiastically.

BACK AT OMEGA

I volunteer the next summer season at Omega. Swan Song and I continue to spend time together intimately, but we have new challenges. A pattern begins to emerge. She defines us as being friends again. But really, whenever we are together, we grow more and more intimate. I believe that after we have been apart for a spell, Swan Song feels remorse. It's a vicious cycle. I feel drawn in close and pushed away like a yoyo. My heart and mind are sent mixed messages. In reality, she doesn't want to acknowledge our love and affection as a relationship. My existence within her world feels unstable and ungrounded.

As an individual, Chief Thunder Cloud has power and

a certain amount of charisma. I dare believe that she might be more in love with what he offers her: his image of power, the type of spiritual work she revels in, access to a community of like-minded friends, the security of a man and his home, and travel to foreign countries. She certainly wants the world to acknowledge her as Chief Thunder Cloud's partner.

"This above all: to thine own self be true, And it must follow, as the night the day, Thou canst not then be false to any man." — William Shakespeare, Polonius

In some ways, my desire to be with her has turned into a blind obsession. I can't bring myself to terminate our affair. In part, because she gave me her heart, then her body, accompanied by her soul. With the gift of her body, our spirits did merge and I have had a taste of her soul. That bond cannot be easily retracted or shaken off. Besides, she savors being together and continues to furnish hope.

It leads me to set an intention to be a loving friend who will understand and serve her. Now, I have made it my business to get to know her deepest desires, the subtle nuances in her facial expressions and body language, and the simple pleasures that she enjoys. I become her humble servant. I get to know her routines. She tells me she is grateful to have a friend that cares. During my errands, I pick up chocolate and iced coffee for her. I actually enjoy doing little things, like turning on the light in her tent before she comes home. I don't want her to fumble around in the dark. To my surprise, it has become a satisfying way to express how I care.

We talk about our commitment as friends. We agree to communicate openly, be intimate, and touch, but neither of us wants to be sexual while at Omega. We continue to have fun by spending time playing games like chess and ping-pong. But the most cherished part of our friendship is the time we set aside for healing. This includes giving each other massages and encouragement by praying together.

Once she grabbed me as I came out of the dining hall and pulled me into the bushes. She said, "I really like praying with you. I want to pray right now." We often prayed together in the mornings but had not today. She likes it. We both know that there is power in our prayers. They manifest easily because our hearts are wide-open and in unison. We hold so much love for each other. I wonder, has she ever considered our being a perpetual couple? I know she would experience immense spiritual growth, warm-hearted intimacy, and her soul would rest securely. She will never know these things if she dares not to wade out into the deep water where love flows.

I meet with the councilors available for staff at Omega. I am still seeking to make sense of the whole triangle relationship. It's not happening. My counselor points out that the man Swan Song is living with has been her and my spiritual teacher. This creates a whole new complicated dynamic. Generally, in a student and teacher relationship, the student attempts to seek approval and desires to please the teacher. If it carries over into a personal relationship, it becomes codependency. I don't want to speculate about their relationship. It's all getting more perplexing. I believe that Swan Song has, in many ways, found some spiritual growth from her time with Chief Thunder Cloud.

Chapter 10

The Buildup to the Showdown

E velyn Lim, Intuitive Consultant of Singapore, shares the following information about the Akashic records.

"The Akashic Records refer to a database of every word, thought or action that is stored energetically and encoded in a non-physical plane of existence. They are said to contain the information of every Soul or Being in the cosmos. The Records are continually updated, with each new thought, word or action that every Soul or entity makes. The Akashic Records therefore contain the energetic prints about the origination and journey of every Soul through its lifetimes. They are embedded with information about your previous lifetimes, your Soul Origination, current life lessons and your purpose. You will meet with lessons that will be provided again and again, until you have gained mastery.

"The records are accessed through being in a deep state of relaxation or meditation. Anyone can have the same access to the Akashic Records. It's like having an internet access to the same database of information. In reality, no special powers or abilities are needed to get into the Akashic Records. The same records are accessible by the subconscious mind, through dreams, intuitive and esoteric exercis-

*es. However, a cluttered mind, ego, little connection
with one's Higher Self and a lack of trust in one's
divine power are hindrances that an Akashic Record reader needs to overcome first. It's only when
there is complete harmony between the conscious,
subconscious or superconscious that Truth from the
Akashic Records can be determined.*

*"One of the most famous of Akashic Record read-
ers is the late American psychic Edgar Cayce (1877-
1945). He has been called the "sleeping prophet," the
"father of holistic medicine," and is about the most
documented psychic of the 20th century. He has done
readings on more than 10,000 topics. Other famous
personalities who have accessed the Akashic Records
include Nostradamus, Rudolph Steiner, Mary Baker
Eddy and Emmanuel Swedenborg."* [2]

There is one spiritual intuitive who works at Omega
and offers Akashic readings for clients. Her name is Krystal
Baal. She has glistening, blond, shoulder-length hair and a
smile that covers her face. Her skin emanates softness. She
is all about having fun. I am also able to view past lives
through the Akashic records. I am self-taught in retrieving
and interpreting them. I offer Krystal and another spiritual
intuitive a session. Afterwards, they confirm that I am receiving and interpreting authentically.

Just for fun, Krystal reads my past lives. She is one of
the few people who know of my affection for Swan Song.
She says, "I have never seen so many past lives intersect.
You and she go way back." I am excited about being together with her for so many lifetimes. Then as a friend, she says.
"I suggest that you end it with Swan Song." I feel disappointed. That is not what I want to hear. But she is probably
right. I am sitting on a powder keg, playing with matches.

PAST LIVES

When I journey to the Akashic Records, I start by diving into the ocean. There is a big white shark, my protective guardian, which swims around me. I dive to the bottom of the ocean. There I see a large, wooden chest that contains some significant item, like a gemstone, a key, or a star. I swim to the shore and come out of the water. I walk down a street of Roman courthouse structures with tall, white columns. There are seven different buildings all having to do with past, present, or future lives.

I go up the white stone steps of the Akashic Record Library and inside. Behind the counter are two Egyptian-looking attendants. One has the body of a woman with the head of a fox. I offer them a basket of fruit. They love peaches and watermelons. With their permission, I request a book from my past life or that of another person. They escort me to the appropriate aisle. I find the book I am seeking. I will often request to see where one life intercepts with another. When I open the book, symbols appear such as a pine tree, a sled, and two children. I interpret the symbols and in my mind's eye it creates a visual story. In nearly every past life Swan Song and I have lived, we found each other. And there are hundreds of books. It is true!

In one of our more recent past lives, we were brother and sister around ages eight and ten, living in India. A landslide covered the schoolhouse we were in. We were both trapped down low, but could move around among the rubble to be near each other. We held hands in the darkness. Although we both succumbed to starvation, we found comfort in each other that took away the fear of death. Now, in our present lives, we both keep a food stash, even when meals are provided. With this insight into our past life, we can better understand, and if we choose, change our behavior in this life. Maybe we don't need to hoard apples, almonds, and chocolate.

Swan Song vividly recalls a past life when we were sorcerers. When she talks about it, I feel it's during the medieval period in England. As in this life, we both have the power to heal and wield magic. She recalls the time I cast a horrendous spell. Most likely, I had used my power in an attempt to win her over. Whatever it was I did, it left such a deep impression that she has not forgotten it in this life.

PAST WIVES

I request to be shown books relevant to Swan Song and my lives intersecting. I am shown three of our past lives where we were involved in a relationship. In the first past life, I read the symbols of a rabbit, coyote, moon, stars, and a cooking pot. Each symbol represents an important part of our past life. One by one, I focus on the symbols. Then the life vision it represents appears.

This is not the first life in which Chief Thunder Cloud and I have encountered each other with Swan Song's love and affection being the central conflict. In this one, Swan Song is living in a Native American village with Chief Thunder Cloud. He is a husband of good standing, and together they have many kids. They multiply like...ah...*rabbits*. I live in another Native tribe and meet her at a trade gathering. At first sight, our hearts are drawn toward each other. I secretly travel to visit her village at dusk. We make passionate love in the *moonlight* in the woods behind the canyon edge. When she returns to her husband, her face reveals instantly her betrayal. As I am running back towards my village, there are beautiful sparkling *stars* filling the night sky. It's a feeling of being young as my heart beats madly, overflowing with the joy of being alive and in love. Then the *coyotes* start to howl, just as they did in this life when I was forced away from her tent. It's the cry of our hearts for each other. We both hear it and know it.

Now Chief Thunder Cloud has a dilemma: he could ask her to leave or stay; it's his right to decide. He chooses to have her stay and deal with the hardship surrounding the situation. He wants Swan Song to continue her role for the sake of his family and the tribe. He needs a wife to keep the *cooking pot* full of stew. A year later, we spot each other again at the trade gathering. This time Chief Thunder Cloud keeps her close. We have no more physical interactions, just a glance, a memory, and a longing.

After viewing this first past life, I close the book and leave the hall of records. I walk back to the shore, preparing to swim back. Before I touch a foot to the water, something unheard of in this spirit realm happens. Chief Thunder Cloud comes out of the water. He is rather upset and yells, "You have stolen her from me in three different lives!"

Needless to say, there has been tension between Chief Thunder Cloud and me regarding Swan Song for a few past lives. Clearly, it's still not resolved. Once he cooled down, Chief Thunder Cloud and I actually had a discussion about her. True to his nature, he even suggested a few pointers about how to get along with Swan Song. He says, "When she gets upset, just be silent." Perhaps, somewhere deep in his soul, Chief Thunder Cloud knows that Swan Song and I have a special bond of love that has endured through many lifetimes.

I return to the Akashic records to read our second past life together. Swan Song is married again but to a different man. We meet during a heavy snowstorm in a Scandinavian town. She is sniffling with a cold, so I offer to bring her home with my horse and sleigh. I bring her back to my home, not hers. I make a warm fire. Perhaps from this past life, she has taken with her a romantic affection for fires. She does not make it back to her home until the next morning. Upon her return, her husband uses a horsewhip to punish her. Once again she is punished for being with me.

The third life encounter goes way back to when we were living in caves. She is out gathering food and is attacked and eaten by a saber-toothed tiger. I watch it from a distance, but it's too late and there is nothing I can do. It's devastating for me. My unrestrained primitive heart wails out in agony for her. This may explain why from early on, it has been hard for me to be away from her for long. It seems we have left each other with an unexpected death, mine with the bear and hers with the saber-toothed tiger.

THE BUILDUP

Once while walking to a yoga class at Omega, Swan Song asks me out of the blue, "Will you protect me?" I reply, "Yes." But I ask myself. *Why is she scared? What do I need to protect her from?*

She actually is safe, but for her to *feel* safe means something completely different. I believe she wants to know that she can fully relax and feel secure in my presence. Obviously, she will not be physically hurt while she is with me. But women have a variety of ways that allow them to feel psychologically and emotionally safe. I know the true nature of my beloved. Being held or touched brings her the most comfort, along with cozy blankets and pillows, praying together, being with friends, or sipping a hot cup of tea.

Early one morning, Swan Song slips into my tent in her pajamas and crawls under the covers beside me. We both know that Chief Thunder Cloud will arrive at Omega later that day. Why do we meet at such a precarious moment?

"Those who restrain desire do so because theirs is weak enough to be restrained."
— *William Blake, The Marriage of Heaven and Hell*

Since being back, we have discussed the topic of our lovemaking in Costa Rica. Initially, she said, "It worked for me." It led me to believe that she enjoyed our lovemaking. But today when it comes up in our conversation, she refers to it as "a mistake." I can't believe she considers our lovemaking a mistake. It hurts my pride to even consider our making love as a mistake. The most I will admit is that maybe she is right, and maybe I am wrong. But in all honesty, I don't regret it. There have been so few lovers in my life with whom I was capable of expressing my love in a healthy, wholesome way. Oh Lord, allow me to keep one shred of pride. *No!* I hear you. We both made a mistake.

It feels awful when she leaves my warm bed to go pack her bags to stay with Chief Thunder Cloud in his cabin. Whenever he comes to Omega, it is her ritual to go and spend her nights in a cabin with him. When it is time to depart, she becomes instantly cold. The sudden leaping from my bed to his feels nasty. I want to retain integrity if I am to be with her. Now I am sucked back into being a part of this devious affair. Our being together is once again taking place behind his back. We are being as sneaky as we were before Costa Rica.

During the times Chief Thunder Cloud visits, I no longer exist in Swan Song's world. When he is present, she suddenly becomes his humble and devoted servant. This is the chameleon side of her I have never met. As soon as he drives away, I reappear and my beloved changes back into the woman I know and love.

On one rare occasion, while Chief Thunder Cloud is on the campus, she breaks through this barrier to show affection towards me. I am staying in her tent and she comes under the guise of needing a pillow and fetching toothpaste for him. We embrace each other while lying in her bed for what seems like an hour. It is clear to me that she needs to be held. Although she ensures me that he would not visit her tent, the thought of him making a sudden appearance makes me nervous. I feel that uncomfortable, on-edge feeling. I imagine it is emotionally draining for her to hold space for two men on the same campus. There are other nights when Swan Song feels haunted by the possibility that Chief Thunder Cloud will suddenly appear and find us together in her tent. For this reason, she is most at ease when we are at our camping spot a short drive away from Omega.

OUR CAMPING SPOT

Tucked into the woods off the hiking trail around a quaint pond, is a three-sided lean-to made of large, pine logs. There is a stone fire pit directly in front of it and a weathered picnic table off to the side. There are pine planks on the floor and it all smells like pine inside. Someone had used a knife to carve, in old English script, five of the seven deadly sins. On the three surrounding walls are the words GREED, WRATH, and ENVY. PRIDE hangs overhead. LUST finds its place on the floor directly in front of our tent opening. How appropriate a reminder. (If you're racking your brain, gluttony and sloth are the two missing deadly sins.)

The opening faces toward the pond, which is no more than 25 feet away. In the late afternoon, the ducks come in for a landing as a marmalade sunset engulfs the horizon. At night the frogs near the shore create a chorus of peeps and chirps with the exceptional, resounding, deep croak from a bullfrog.

When I am here by myself or awaiting Swan Song, I always find peace looking at the reflections in the pond. There are tall grasshopper-green grasses and gnarly tree limbs half submerged in the water. They make an ideal place for the turtles to rest while bathing in the last glistening rays. If I move suddenly or a hiker passes on the trail, the turtles plop back into the water. A moment later, a head slowly appears and stretches out before its cautious return.

During our first autumn together, we claim this site as our camping spot. We stick a red prayer flag filled with tobacco high in a tree overhanging the pond directly in front of our camping spot. When we return the next summer, we are glad to see it still hanging, though it has faded. There is an old John-Deere-green hand pump not far away. It provides our drinking water. We take turns pumping the handle as the other rinses the dishes or takes a quick shower.

From near the hand pump, we can watch the smoke from our fire and look down the length of the pond. We gather firewood together before dark. Swan Song loves to sit and stare into the fire. On the cold, fall nights, we are cozy and sleep deeply as we hold each other beneath my buffalo robe. She always sleeps on her left side. I spoon her. If I'm not close enough, she wiggles herself backwards to fill in the crevice. My right arm rests comfortably upon her waist. My hand cups her small, soft fingers. The nostalgic smell of smoke mixes with the smell of the buffalo leather and the scent of our skin. At night when we first bed down, a silhouette from the flames dances on the side of our tent. Later we hear the crackling and popping of the fire as it peters down to form red-hot coals.

We both cherish our favorite camping spot. In the fall, we wear jeans and cuddly, wool sweaters. I savor the comfort of her leaning her head onto my chest while we lie on a woven blanket in the sun. It's as much about the warm, glowing feelings of being together in nature, as being in love.

The timelessness of the breeze gently blows the leaves. I gaze at her watching the clouds. She notices and smiles, returning my glance.

THE MEDICINE WHEEL

"Native American traditions were not based on a fixed set of beliefs or on an interpretation of sacred writings, but on the knowledge of the rhythm of life which they received through the observation of Nature. All of Nature expresses itself in circular patterns. This can be seen in something as small and simple as a bird's nest as well as in things much greater such as the cycle of the seasons or the cycle of life (birth, death, rebirth). And therefore, to Native American peoples, the circle or wheel represents Wakan-Tanka ("the Great Everything" or Universe) and also one's own personal space or personal universe.

"In Native American belief, the cardinal directions are linked to great Powers, or intelligent forces, whose energy (or Medicine) can be harnessed. The directions can be charted on a circular map, the Medicine Wheel, which can enable one to come into alignment with these spiritual powers and absorb something of them.

"Each direction on the Wheel constitutes a path of self-realization and self-initiation into the mysteries of life which can lead you to the very core of your being where you can make contact with your own High Self. Each path can help you to acquire the knowledge to work changes that will put meaning and purpose into your life, bringing enlightenment and fulfillment." [3]

During our second season together, we build a Native American medicine wheel on the moss a few feet away from the pond. We use slate rocks to create a circular border. The circle represents the sacred outer boundary of the earth, often referred to as the sacred hoop. Then we create horizontal and vertical lines through the circle's center to divide it into four quarters. They represent the four directions and all the other correlating components from the circle of life.

The National Library of Medicine states,

"Different tribes interpret the Medicine Wheel differently. Each of the Four Directions (East, South, West, and North) is typically represented by a distinctive color, such as black, red, yellow, and white. The directions can also represent:
- *Stages of life: birth, youth, adult (or elder), death*
- *Seasons of the year: spring, summer, winter, fall*
- *Aspects of life: spiritual, emotional, intellectual, physical*
- *Elements of nature: fire (or sun), air, water, and earth*
- *Animals: Eagle, Bear, Wolf, Buffalo and many others*
- *Ceremonial plants: tobacco, sweet grass, sage, cedar"* [4]

We are always barefoot when within the medicine wheel. We walk in a clockwise, or "sun-wise" direction. In the center, we keep sage and a few white eagle feathers, standing upright. The eagle feather is a sign of the power our Creator has over everything.

It's the way we made the medicine wheel together with love, that stirs up my sentimental feelings. There is more power in the harmony that exists between a man and a woman then we tend to acknowledge. Of course, there is power in the Native Medicine, but love multiplies it exponentially. I brought Althea's husband, Huck Finn, whom I truly respect, to visit the medicine wheel while we were on a biking expedition. Huck just sat barefoot on a log in front of it and meditated. He could feel the love, the power, and the magic inherent in it. Then he was catapulted into an intoxicated state of bliss. I know what he felt; it was our love. The love that my beloved and I share is not of this world.

THE CONFLICTS

One Friday, Swan Song suggests that I go during the day to place my tent on our camping spot to ensure we reserve it before the weekend. She says, "I have a feeling you had better go set up your tent so we get our spot." I am reluctant. She says, "Chief Thunder Cloud listens and follows my intuition." Her statement was a low jab. I feel resentment, but begrudgingly go and set up my tent. When I return in the evening, my tent has been stolen.

She has a spare tent that we use. The stolen tent is not a big deal. What is more important is that she now knows not to treat me or expect me to react and operate in a manner similar to Chief Thunder Cloud. It is normal to draw from our past relationship experiences, but it can also be misleading.

Swan Song and I experience inner growth when we are being vulnerable with one another. I never want to repress what she says and have always encouraged her to be open. No doubt her claim to be available and unattached before her visit to Costa Rica should have made me wary, but somehow her charm and beauty override it. In general, she is honest with me. While we are discussing a couple's relationship retreat at Omega, she exclaims, "This is the kind of relationship work I want to be doing with Chief Thunder Cloud!"

I say, "You mean what we are already doing?"

She responds, "Yes!"

The rawness of her being *that* honest wears on me. She

has no hesitation to speak about a future with Chief Thunder Cloud in my presence. Once she even said, "It doesn't really matter which man I choose as long as I keep working on a relationship."

Eventually, Swan Song finds compassion, and says, "I know my actions have hurt you. I don't want to keep hurting you."

I respond, "Well, one thing you *can* do is stop talking about Chief Thunder Cloud when we are together."

Swan Song clearly begins to shut me out during these intense emotional moments when Chief Thunder Cloud is around. Once while he is on campus, I return to Omega and see her on the path by the café. She looks around and gives me a quick, nervous hug. I begin to walk with her along the path. Her fear that Chief Thunder Cloud will appear erupts. In anger, she shouts, "Go away! I can't have you near me."

Around this time, our stress had reached a pinnacle. Later on, I realize our trust has grown solid enough to withstand expressing real emotions like anger without holding back. Studies show that women who deal with anger indirectly or attempt to suppress it are more likely to experience depression, anxiety, and physical complaints than women who are more direct. There is freedom in being able to express a full array of emotions. We have always been able to forgive each other after a spat because our love allows it.

After Chief Thunder Cloud departs, I immediately go to her tent. She is physically and emotionally exhausted, but that does not matter. It is my turn to express my exasperation at being diminished. I go into her tent and fall upon my knees. I tell her, and express with tears streaming down my cheeks, how humiliated she made me feel. I do not deserve to be cast aside like a piece of trash when Chief Thunder Cloud is present.

Afterwards, whenever possible, I make arrangements to

leave the Omega campus when Chief Thunder Cloud comes for his visits. But Omega is a small campus and eventually we meet, face to face.

THE SHOWDOWN AT OMEGA CORRAL

When first revealed, the truth does not always make life easier. After it has been withheld for months, the impact is compounded. Chief Thunder Cloud knows about Swan Song and me being together in Costa Rica. Even though I am glad the cat is out of the bag, so to speak, it makes my next encounter with him intensely uncomfortable and downright despicable.

The Omega dining hall is filled with 300 - 400 people that are a combination of volunteers, retreat participants, and spiritual teachers. For those who live and breathe in this community, the dining hall is a sensitive and energetic place where you must stay grounded so as not to wash away in the energetic flow of chatter. One has to step mindfully down the main aisle as the kitchen volunteers, in blue aprons with handkerchiefs on their heads, bustle back and forth, carrying silver trays loaded with organic veggies, through swinging, saloon-style doors.

In the main corridor are two food lines that converge into a giant T-shaped formation. Each branch flows into a station on the left and right with four milk dispensers hanging down like the teats on a cow. There are coffee dispensers at chest level, with red handles that extend out resembling slot machines. Against the wall is an assortment of fruit with a display of layered rocks stacked behind it. If this were a town in the Wild West, the innocent bystanders would have ducked behind the rocks when the shots started firing. On the countertops, bouquets of tall, wild grasses hide innocent-looking flowers that sit prettily as they watch the flurry of commotion below. The participants, carrying white plates and bowls filled with salads and chickpea gumbo, meander down both sides of the food line and overflow into the center arrangement like tumbleweeds in a dust storm. They bounce against the back wall or gather in small clusters before sliding over to fetch a drink at one of the stations.

It's high noon when I enter the back door of the dining hall after eating outside. I know without glancing up that Chief Thunder Cloud is in the room. The air is thick. We are about to have our first uncomfortable encounter since he uncovered our forbidden secret. The fact that I now know that he knows makes it even worse. I step out into the clearing at one end of the dining hall. The room becomes deadly silent. The floor clears of all its participants, as if they know there will be a showdown. One lone participant looks up from filling a glass of milk and scurries nervously away. In my left hand I have my dirty plate, and a fork and a knife in my right trigger-finger hand. I peer down the long, striped lines on the wooden floor that lead directly to the far end of hall where Chief Thunder Cloud stands. He has just dropped off his dirty dishes at the counter. He turns his boots to face in my direction.

I take a breath and tell myself, *Stand tall. Stay strong. Wait until you see the whites of his eyes. Let him react first.*

A participant in the corner strums an eerie twang on his guitar. The showdown has begun. Chief Thunder Cloud starts to walk towards me and I towards him. There is no turning back or changing our paths. This is not a time to waver or show weakness. I feel every breath. My heartbeat pounds in my eardrums. We walk as if in slow motion. As he passes a bowl of oranges, crazy thoughts enter my mind: *If he grabs an orange and pegs it at me, can I deflect it with my plate? If he takes a swing at me, should I duck or block it?*

We both have our arms dangling at our sides, ready to draw our pistols, as the timeless spiritual showdown over Swan Song begins. Fifty feet away now. No backing down. Our paths are going to cross. Twenty feet away now. In slow motion, the details become clear. I can see the whites of his eyes. I lift my eyebrows in a gesture of acknowledgement to this man, who was once my friend and spiritual teacher. He stares straight ahead with a cold, rattlesnake stare. I hold ground anxiously, as if I were the prey standing before the rattlesnake with its head raised, ready to strike. I hold my breath; this is the inevitable moment I have been waiting for and wanting to avoid. We pass each other like two giant cargo ships that pass so close they scrape the paint off the metal with a screech. Both of us are left shaken but still standing.

I stumble and stagger away towards Eric the Viking, who in that moment had swooped in for a plateful of chocolate chip cookies. He says, "How are you doing, man?" Maybe he sensed my desolate pain. He gives me a long hug. He was a refuge for me in this battle-scarred, barren land.

He says, "Wow, I really needed that hug!"

He has no idea what just happened, but he held my soul for a moment, when I could no longer bear it. Our hug welds back together the cracks that formed in my heart. I attempt to express my gratitude to him for being there in that moment, but fall short.

He laughs and says, "I gain my emotional nurturing from eating a mountain of chocolate chip cookies."

Chapter 11

Sacrum Meltdown II

Isit alone in Swan Song's tent. It will be the last time I am in her tent this season. I absorb the unwanted fact that I will be leaving her soon. We have spent most of our free time together as if we were inseparable. During our moments together, time nearly stopped. But then again, two months passed as quickly as a wink. I look at the blankets and pillows on her neatly-made bed. We spent precious time lounging on top of them, sharing the mundane and outlandish details from our days. She bubbled up when she retold her interactions. I enjoyed listening. It became a self-indulgent treat.

When we are physically together, our intimacy grows. When we are apart, it's never the same. We agree to communicate once a week, or was it once a month? I forget. It felt like a tedious negotiation. It doesn't really matter on some level. Regardless, once I leave, our level of intimacy will fade. I fear our inevitable parting. There are deeper emotional and psychological implications and I don't pretend to understand them all. I just don't want to be away from her. It's unsettling. Her soothing smile and her internal rhythm are like a cozy blanket on a chilly night. And it's about to be yanked away.

When I slowly walk away from her tent, my sacrum begins to tremble and quake. I place my right hand on my pelvis and my left hand on the sacrum region of my back. There is no holding it back! The internal earthquake begins to erupt. I am going into a full-blown relapse: my second sacrum meltdown. I drop my bags at my side and stare straight ahead. Instantaneously, the harness of muscles around my sacrum starts to wind as tightly as a winch with steel cables. *It is out of control. I can't turn it off.* Red lights flash. I attempt to hit the emergency button. No success. My response is to hunch over and curl up. My skeletal structure *cracks* and *pops* as it dislocates my spine, sacrum, and ribs. Then it creaks to a cringing halt.

At this point, I am messed up, but when I am with Swan Song, I feel completely loved. She is the one I want beside me when I am suffering. Even the thought of death is not so bad, if she is holding my hand. But the tragic thought of not being with her is enough to mess up my fragile world. I can barely walk and I am in no condition to drive away. *Have I become a co-dependent marshmallow?*

At Omega, when you are in a bind, somebody just appears at the perfect moment. My fairy-like friend, Blossom, instantly vaporizes from a cloud of magic dust. I hobble down with her to a cabin by the lake, where there is a massage table. She brings some relief to my muscles through her soothing touch. Nonetheless, my sacrum and ribs remain dislocated.

Blossom compassionately explains, "This healing crisis stems from your emotions. It's all about Swan Song."

I don't want to admit it, but I know she is right. I am shocked that my emotions have the power to instantaneously incapacitate my body. During the tremor, my mind left my body. It's standing on the breakdown lane on the interstate in L.A. watching rush-hour traffic zoom past. Meanwhile, my body is crying out to be touched by Swan Song. Something deep inside, beyond my awareness, is afraid to leave her.

Suddenly, Swan Song appears with a smile. Beside the

lake, she carefully sets out a blanket in the sun. I slowly lie down on it. She starts by softly massaging my tight legs and back muscles. Then I hobble back to the massage table in the cabin for the remainder of her massage. When she is done, she lightly holds my feet for a moment. I am lying face up on the massage table. She skips to the left side of the table and swings her leg up and over like she is getting on a horse. Instead, she lies down with her full body in contact with mine. She ends with a big, long hug on top of me. I utter out...*Awhhhh!* This is not what I expected, but it's what I needed. What I desired more than anything was to have her full body and heart close to mine. My body may still be in pain, but my emotions and spirit are being nurtured.

During my dinners at Omega, friends listen and support me with hugs. I recover enough after three days to drive to my friend's home in Pennsylvania. I call him Cowboy, for a good reason. He used to work at Miracle Mountain Ranch. That is probably where he learned to crack whips. He has been the main attraction at a few western events. It sounds like a gunshot when cracked properly. It actually breaks the sound barrier.

Cowboy rented a room in the same house while we both went to Liberty University. One of the first nights, he charged into my room wearing tights and a jester's hat, wielding a long, moon-shaped sword. I burst out laughing! We are the best of friends. I stay with him a few weeks as my sacrum heals. We often share what is happening in our relationships. He listens patiently to my agonizing trials with Swan Song.

SPIRITUAL WARFARE

During my drive down, I listened to a recording of Freud. He explained how sexual dysfunction is caused by our emotions getting tangled up in our sexuality. His remedy is to do non-sexual regressive work to express anxiety, aggression, and other emotions related to sexually traumatic events.

Caring for the Heart counseling uses a similar technique of regressing to the original trauma through visualization, and then Jesus comes to heal the trauma. My emotions are entangled in my sacrum area. It feels like a ball of cold spaghetti tied up in knots. My issues could be more sexually related than I realize. I am beginning to understand that I have an intimacy and attachment disorder. I can't continue to aggravate this unhealthy pattern with Swan Song. I need to heal it.

As a counselor trained in Caring for the Heart techniques, I begin to work on myself. I use them as a weapon to break apart the spiritual bindings of my past traumatic sexual entanglements. I arm myself with prayers, a Bible, and worship music before charging into battle. It lasts for seven days. I address the sex I had with any women other than my wife and all my deviant sexual acts: pornography, strip clubs, and sexual fantasies. I repent these acts. I call back parts of my soul that were stuck clinging to past sexual partners.

My first battle was when I was 13 years old. I had my first sexual encounter when a so-called friend molested me. During this session, I pray to be shown the visual effects it had on my heart. In my heart, I see a pitted, black crater. I go back and relive what I felt during that encounter. It's a mixture of pleasure and fear. Then, my insides lock up. During this session, Jesus comforts my 13-year-old self.

I ask Jesus, "Why were you not able to stop it?"

Jesus replies, "Men have free will and Satan was given authority to rule over certain aspects on the earth. I have the authority to heal what has been damaged by him."

Jesus sits a foot away from me in a chair. He says, "Give

Me your pain."

It's my choice to hold on to the pain or give it to Him. The pain is not serving me. I start by giving Him a flake of the pain from my pocket. Then I begin to pull out my pitted, black-crater heart and hand it all over to Him.

As I am doing this, I yell, "It hurts! It hurts! It hurts!"

I worry that Jesus or somebody else will receive this horrible pain.

He says, "The pain will not be given to Me or anybody else."

He places my pitted, black-crater heart in a plastic beach pail and kicks it far out into the white light. Then, I give Him a red-hot metal bar that is in my spine and a collar that is around my throat.

I was told by my perpetrator to keep it all a secret.

Jesus explains, "What this man did to you was wrong."

Jesus gives me a new heart. I can feel the warmth inside me. It's a bright pink heart that is bouncy and flexible.

Jesus says, "I love you."

I now know that even if you are molested, the perpetrator can never touch that part inside of you that is Holy.

JESUS WALKS BESIDE ME

Jesus then reveals a past experience from when I was eight years old, to show an example of how He is different from my father. At that age, I would run and play for hours without end. While at camp, The Lion would, on occasion, go into the woodshed and come back disguised as a monster. His costume consisted of removing his toupee and brushing his remaining hair on either side straight up. He would become a scary hunchback by placing a pillow under his shirt on his upper back. He wore a set of plastic fangs over his teeth and would walk with a deformed limp in his right leg. Growling and snarling, he chased my siblings and me in circles around the kitchen table.

In his way, he was being affectionate, and we all had fun. Even though he was playing, this game was about our being afraid of the monster my father had become.

Jesus says, "I will walk beside you. If you run, I will run next to you. I will always be with you. I offer healing to the people that come to Me."

In my experience, healing occurs when the receiver is ripe. It requires an intervention from God, but the actual format that the healing manifests is of lesser importance. God has many channels and people who act as His instruments.

At the end of my session, Jesus sends a beam of white light that shines on my sacrum. It melts some of the tightness. Healing occurs though subtle shifts. I acknowledge the forward step I have made.

Chapter 12

Finding a Hero

Istay in a cabin in Virginia near Yogaville for the next few months. I focus on getting stronger and dedicate my energy towards rebuilding my body. I receive regular chiropractic appointments to adjust my ribs and sacrum back into their proper locations. I get a weekly massage, attend Integral Yoga and Zumba dance classes, swim, hang on an inversion table, and start to lift weights twice a week to build up my strength.

I feel the urge to write more of my book, but when I take the time to listen deep inside, it's not the right time to write. I need to relax and allow my back and neck muscles time to heal before I attempt to sit and write. I don't write one word of my book during my time at the cabin. The fastest way for me to heal is in silence. It allows me to quickly get in touch. I pray for guidance on how to deal with the complex issues surrounding my topsy-turvy relationship with Swan Song.

I am silent for ten days. It feeds my spirit and soul. I set the intention to find the hero inside myself. At a yard sale, I buy a series of 1960s movies with Hercules and an array of heroes from *The Odyssey*. In each movie, there is always a villain, usually a battle with man or monster, a defining moment to prove the hero's character, and a beautiful damsel whom instantly falls head-over-heels in love with the hero. Hercules, to my surprise, likes to take naps and lounge around and relax. I think I could handle being a hero in that regard! I can't swing trees around to knock men off their horses like Hercules, but I can find inspiration in the hero's character, strength, and courage.

FOUR QUESTIONS FROM JESUS

Jesus is also my hero. During my silent 10-day retreat, I feel Jesus ask me four questions. They are regarding our relationship and my obedience towards him.

1) Jesus asks, "Do you choose to follow me above all other forms of God?"

I answer, "Yes, but why can't I follow all forms of God?"

Jesus replies, "I want you to choose all of me or none of me!"

In that case, "Yes, I want to choose you, Jesus!"

2) Jesus asks, "If I ask you to read the Bible each day, would you do it?"

I reply, "Yes, I give my highest authority to you. I want to be obedient to your requests."

3) Jesus asks, "Will you live in a community filled with corny people that are devoted to me?"

Many of my friends are Christians. They are decent people, whom I love and respect. Once I get to know them, they aren't that corny.

I say, "Yes, I would live in a community of corny people devoted to you."

4) His last question is the toughest. Jesus asks, "If I asked you to let go of Swan Song, would you do that for me?"

I start to cry and yell out, "NO! That is a mean question. I will not give up the woman I love for you."

Jesus says, "Now that you are being real, we can start a relationship."

I begin to contemplate the last question. If God has a sovereign plan that determines everything that happens in this universe, then being with Swan Song is out of my control. I believe that God has an individual, detailed plan for my life.

After a few days, I surrender. I let Jesus know, "Yes, if you ask me to let go of Swan Song, then I will do it."

I know that Jesus will not request something of me that is not in my best interest. Mind you, Jesus did not actually make any of those requests. He was checking the state of my heart. He may, in fact, make such requests at a later date, or I might find out that His request is my only option.

SITTING TO MEDITATE ON THE LOG

I ask myself what a hero would do in my situation with Swan Song. I walk out into the woods and sit in the sun on a log to contemplate. How do I feel about Swan Song deep down inside? There is no doubt... I love her. In a relationship I need to feel sparks. Like two magnets placed near each other, they either repel or attract. Swan Song and I certainly feel divine sparks when we are together. I reflect on the closeness we have developed and those actions that strengthen our bond.

She once gave me a bookmark that shows a walking path in the forest. It read, "It doesn't matter where you go in life... It's who you have beside you." Her written words like these and her actions lead me to believe she wants us to be together. I think I know how she feels about me, but her actions and words are often contradictory.

Our health and beauty diminish as we get older. But in my eyes, Swan Song gets more beautiful each day. Consider her bizarre sleeping rituals. She likes the bed tucked in, with lots of covers, and each morning she meticulously makes her bed. While sleeping, she puts in earplugs, places a scarf over her face, inserts a knee pillow, and cuddles with a dagger-size stone of selenium. She says it emits healing vibrations. That's not the worst part. Lately, she has begun a strange new ritual. She sleeps with duct tape over her mouth. This way she is forced to breathe through her nose. How would I kiss such a horrid creature good night? Should I remove the duct tape or just kiss it? My point is that her inner beauty is what matters; her external, daytime beauty is a bonus.

During this last season at Omega, Swan Song has grown to have more integrity in her relationships. I believe the primary reason is that she has to teach other women about relationships and it has forced her to look at herself. This was an area of concern, but now it's a reason to find her more appealing. I know that neither of us is perfect; we both have our "stuff" that comes up. When it does, we take time to sit down face to face. We really listen and share from our hearts. I actually look forward to our arguments because I know we will resolve our problems with kindness. It draws us closer. Together, we find spiritual growth and expand to become the best versions of ourselves. As part of this process, I get to understand more about her needs, interests, fears, goals, dreams, and what brings her joy and sadness. I want her to live in a way that will bring her happiness, whether we are together or apart.

What we are experiencing in essence is a "conscious relationship." That means we came together with the intention to find emotional and spiritual growth as individuals and a couple. We allow the other space to fully express and feel. Even if at times those feelings trigger something within the other. We focus more on embodying love and being vulnerable than the outcome of our relationship. We certainly have experienced more growth together than we could have alone. But at this point, I can't continue with Swan Song unless there is a shift to allow integrity to be at the core of our relationship.

In the past, I have prayed very specifically for the qualities I sought in a wife. She needs to communicate openly and honestly, and be dedicated to the relationship even when times get tough. This means being kind, compassionate, understanding, and forgiving, even when it's hard to do. She should have her own life and friends. She should not take life too seriously, because I like to laugh with my mate. It's best if we are both on the same spiritual path or aligned with similar values.

Once, after I prayed for a wife, God whispered, "You will find this woman. She is going to be far more magnificent than you can ever imagine!" It could be Swan Song. I am not sure.

While sitting on that log, I get in touch with my heart. There is a strong desire in my heart to be with Swan Song. We are soul mates. We were inexplicably drawn together. In her presence, I feel a sense of peace, calmness, and joy. She fills my heart. When I think of her, it begins to melt and burn. She has told me that she has had similar feelings. When I am near her, I feel divine light shine from within her, and it makes me glow.

A hero will express how he feels to the woman he loves. He will take action. I do not want to let Swan Song, whom I adore, slip out of my life. My heart needs to express to Swan Song how I feel about her. There is no way to capture all the love I feel in words. I must find a symbolic way to let her know. It's time for my heart to override my mind. I am ready to make a hero's stand.

I decide, sitting on that log, that the best way I can show

Swan Song how much I love her is to ask her to marry me. In a bizarre way, it makes sense, given our crazy situation. This step would allow us to break away completely from the web of deception. Swan Song has had the past twenty months to make a decision about which man she wants in her life. Her choice has been to use both men to fulfill different needs. But now, all three of us are caught like buzzing flies in a sticky web. We are just waiting for the spider — the spider that has already begun to devour me from the inside out.

If I propose marriage, then Swan Song will *need* to make a decision. I take into consideration that she has told me she is not available for a relationship. But maybe that is on a superficial layer, because she considers herself spoken for. Deep down I believe she loves me, to the depths of the sea. Marriage has a way of bringing love to a whole new level. I want her to experience marriage with a man who will treat her with kindness, love, and respect. She never received that in her first marriage. She deserves it. This could be a second chance for us both. If she chooses to marry me, she will be endorsing our love in front of our friends and family. This way, all three of us can retain our respect and dignity.

Swan Song has three days of Caring for the Heart counseling sessions scheduled for the fall. I have faith that the counselors, with the help of Jesus, can heal her broken heart. I eagerly await the results. This could give her a whole new perspective on marriage and some of the deeper issues that have surfaced. I decide it's best to place my faith in Jesus. If Swan Song is ready, Jesus can resolve her past marriage issues in three days. I have placed her in the best hands I know. I decide that I will pray for Swan Song each day for two weeks prior to her counseling and all during the actual sessions.

SWAN SONG'S FIRST MARRIAGE

Swan Song had been raised in a Christian household. I believe her father was a pastor. They upheld traditional family values. In her early twenties, she was engaged. Both she and her mother thought her fiancé, Michael, was a real honest-to-goodness angel. She wanted a simple, small wedding. Her mother instead insisted on a large, formal wedding. Her mom, in part, took control of Swan Song's wedding plans. She allowed her mother to do so, even though it was not exactly what she wanted.

On the wedding day, a few hours before the ceremony, her husband-to-be changed his mind. Michael confessed to Swan Song that he did not want to marry her. He wanted to call it all off. The pastor was a family friend. When he found out, he took Michael aside and they had a stern talk.

The pastor told him, in no uncertain terms, "Swan Song is a quality woman. It will be a big mistake if you back out of the wedding now." Under mounting pressure, the groom complied. But he still confided to the pastor that deep down, he did not want to marry her. They went forward with the ceremony. The crowd was waiting, and the ceremony would temporarily evade shame for Swan Song and her family. However, the pastor never even sent in the official wedding certificate. Their marriage never became legal. Michael had become a fallen angel.

To say that Swan Song was devastated after this experience is an understatement. I assume she felt abandoned and disgraced by her incomplete and short-lived marriage. I don't know if I can even call it a marriage. Swan Song was left in a state of miserable disarray. Her husband was like an actor in a Shakespearean tragedy. Her first love had passed her a bottle filled with a poisonous concoction of confusion and deception regarding love and marriage. She had no option but to drink it. The whole audience watched, but only she and a few others knew of the underlying deception. The ceremony ended before it began. A few weeks later, Michael left the scene and boarded a plane to Japan. But the ramifications for Swan Song were deep scars. It is understandable why she has a fear of marriage. She confided in me that she never processed her marriage. I believe many of the issues that stemmed from her first marriage still exist today.

There was nothing any man could ever do that was worse than what had already happened to her. I know that the initial trauma damaged her in some deep ways, and I am truly concerned. I am not a psychoanalyst. But I did focus intently on their scenario and asked God to reveal what He may. What I present is a theory: Swan Song was hurt so deeply that she stopped trusting men. Is it possible that Swan Song's future method of coping with men after the "Fallen Angel" incident was to become deceptive with them? Maybe it's completely subconscious on her part. It seems normal to try to avoid being hurt again after the torment and heartache that Michael inflicted. Even if it meant stretching the truth. In some way, it makes sense that she would treat future men in the same manner that she was treated by Michael. He deceived her. She learned to deceive them. My theory explains why, when I gaze into her eyes, I sense a lack of trust: *It's hard for her to trust a man.*

I hope it will bring some comfort to Swan Song (and others) to know that she is not alone. We have all been rejected, abandoned, or let down. I recognize her situation was a severe calamity, but you can't expect a relationship to exist without its eventually causing some pain in one way or another.

After one is hurt in a relationship, they may attempt to protect themselves by not extending trust. Perhaps a better approach is to extend trust and give people the freedom to make a mistake. The good news is we can all make a conscious decision, starting right now, to trust people again. Trusting people feels better for everyone involved. But we need to accept the fact: *sometimes we will get hurt.*

Recently Swan Song found information on the internet about Michael. He was still living in Japan, apparently happily married, with two kids. Swan Song and her mother wept together when they found out. Swan Song still thought that Michael was meant to be her husband. She was secretly waiting to be his wife. For the past twenty years, she had hoped that her first love would return. Now, it was clearly no longer possible.

TALKING ABOUT MARRIAGE

In her past, Swan Song wanted to honor the sacred bond of marriage. I talk to the Caring for the Heart counselors and they suggest that we discuss marriage in depth before I propose to her. Through my prayers, I had been guided *not* to talk about the possibility of our future together until after her counseling sessions. It would probably bring up her stuff prematurely. Over the past year, we talked about marriage to a limited degree, but never in depth. Because of her past marriage trauma, I consciously make a commitment, deep within my cells, to never abandon her if we do get married. With her, divorce is not an option.

Since we have been apart, I have sent her half a dozen cards that include big references about marriage. These are big hints. She sends me back nice cards, but her prevailing theme is that we are friends, again. But her actions and affection tell me we are more than friends. In her unspoken words she tells me she loves me, over and over. At the very least, after I propose, I will know exactly where she stands. I guess I really don't know. It's still hard to fully accept that she was capable of deceiving me, just like she did all the other men. I still want to feel special; I want to be the exception, so there are places I fear to go. If I dig deeper within myself, I find a layer of denial. I don't dare believe that she doesn't love me as much as I love her. In my own naive way, I believe that if we both make an honorable stand for love and marriage, all the lying demons will be chased away.

She is staying at Omega until the end of October. I attempt to visit her as I pass by on my way back to Vermont. This time could be our moment to talk more in depth about marriage. But she has made plans to go away that weekend.

REALITY CHECK

Before I leap forward, I figure I had better check in with a few wise female friends. This is my reality check. I call my friend Sunshine, whom I greatly respect, and ask what she thinks about my proposal. She tells me, "Follow your heart." Okay.

On my way back to Vermont, I spend a night at Omega. I enter Swan Song's tent and make an elaborate decorative display on her bed with feathers, leaves, and cards. While I am there, Blossom stops by to return a book. I tell her that I plan to propose to Swan Song. I ask for her advice. She says, "Five guys have proposed to me. I knew right away if I wanted to marry them or not. There were a few guys who never proposed, but if they had, I would have said, 'Yes!'"

I feel some encouragement. Blossom suggests that I give Swan Song all the time she needs to make the decision after the proposal. It generally takes her a long time to make big decisions, so I am planning to give her a month or two for this one.

On the bright side, Swan Song and I set a date a month in advance to meet and go on a hike the afternoon after her final counseling session in Vermont. It will be the first time we have been together in a few months. The day after that, she will travel south for over a month to fulfill other commitments, and then she will go to spend Christmas with her parents. This is the *only* time we can be together in the foreseeable future, so this is when I feel I *must* ask her to marry me.

Chapter 13

The Desert Oasis

B efore I propose to Swan Song, I want to make absolutely sure this is all God's will. I ask God for definite confirmation. I have two things that need to happen. First, I need to find the perfect wedding ring for Swan Song. Second, I need the money to buy it. The property taxes on my home in Vermont are due each October. After paying them, I barely have enough gas money to make it back to Vermont from Virginia. My prayer to God for the money to buy this ring is asking for a small miracle.

I want to buy a wedding ring that represents the quality of life I want to share with her. Therefore, it needs to be a brand-new ring. Swan Song is particular about her jewelry. I am searching for a diamond with turquoise stones on either side. Swan Song loves turquoise and wears it often. My heart will know the perfect ring when I see it. At the moment, I am poor financially, but rich with the overflowing joy of love. The possibility of money presenting itself so I can purchase an expensive wedding ring is crazy. But with God and love, anything is possible!

Turquoise is more popular in the Southwest. During my initial search I can't find any diamond rings with it. While travelling up the east coast I visit numerous jewelers, with no success. Then, out of the blue, I find Kokopelli Jewelers in southern New Hampshire. They sell high-quality diamond rings with turquoise, made by Kabana Jewelers in Albuquerque, New Mexico. The owner is a man from Greece named Stavros Eleftheriou. In 1977, he bought a historical missionary church, saying that it had "a good feeling and a blessing inside." It was there that Stavros set up shop and founded his jewelry business. As a tribute to the church's bell tower, he named his company, *Kabana*, which means "bell" in Greek.

I note one ring called the Desert Oasis, with turquoise on either side. Kabana puts in the extra effort, time, and expense to ensure each piece conforms to the highest standards of excellence. Kabana jewelry contains more gold per piece than most jewelry on the market. Thicker pieces result in more durability and safety for the stone inlay. All pieces are hand-polished to ensure a flawless result. I also like this place because each piece is completely manufactured in the U.S.A., while many jewelry manufacturers outsource parts of production to areas such as Southeast Asia. The Desert Oasis has 58 facets. Those are the planed surfaces. This is a high-quality diamond. Holy smokes! Swan Song will love it, but it's damned expensive.

Kabana says they can custom design this engagement ring in the size I need to fit her finger. The first part of my confirmation has been answered. I have found the perfect ring! If I give her this ring, it will show her how I truly feel about her better than words. (Forgive me if I am starting to sound like a diamond ring advertisement.) The next big question is: Can I come up with the money to buy it?

It will take sixteen days for the whole custom process and shipping from New Mexico. They request a thirty percent down payment to place the order. If I can come up with the deposit and the remaining payment a few weeks later, the ring can be in my hand the day before Swan Song and I plan to rendezvous.

I return to Vermont for the next few weeks before our date. The Lamb has been accepted into a senior housing apartment complex. I want to be there to help her move in. I show The Lamb a picture of the Desert Oasis wedding ring and ask if she will loan me the money to put down the deposit. It's practically impossible for her to say "No" when she sees how happy I am. She will gladly embrace Swan Song as her new daughter-in-law. They have met on a few occasions when Swan Song came to visit me at our brick home.

If I sell my junky, ten-year-old car and use all of next month's income, I will have just enough money to buy the Desert Oasis. I spend my remaining time happily staying with family and friends, even though I must sleep on the floor with cushions for a bed. After ten days, my car sells! There is no sacrifice too big. God has fulfilled the second part of the confirmation. Now I have the money I need to buy the Desert Oasis. I am filled with so much joy that I can't stop singing!

DEER CAMP

As a 46 years old, life is a dream. I am a grown man. It has long been a tradition in our family for the men to go to hunting camp during deer season, even if they no longer hunt deer or drink booze. But one does need a doctor's note or a pretty bad hangover to be excused from drinking. As a teenager, it was sort of a rite of passage to go to hunting camp with the men. It was a big deal to get outfitted as a hunter. It's not just about getting a decent hunting rifle with a 3-8x scope and a license. You need to sight in your gun and scope out your hunting ground before the season starts. Some hunters even spread out apples or buy a salt lick. It's illegal. (I never did it, but some of my nameless friends did.) One needs a belt for your bullets and a nice buck knife. You need to carry a rope to drag the deer out, and a compass, even if you don't know how to use it. You need the proper attire: a red wool jacket, an orange cap, long johns, wool socks, and boots rated for 20 degrees below zero. I like a red Styrofoam pillow to sit on for warmth. You have to bring some snacks, like a bag of peanuts and raisins. Part of the fun as a kid was just getting all decked out.

Once I started going to hunting camp, I found there was a lot of jesting. It's okay to call somebody a dumb ass. Your really don't need a reason. You just make one up. Sometimes it is done just to get a reaction. There are a lot of obscene words being tossed around. I guess it makes us feel more like men. It is good for men to hang out. When there's work to be done, like hauling firewood, we all pitch in. It sure feels nice to stand near a wood fire, especially after traipsing around in the cold. Everybody brings some groceries. The wives often make a roast, baked beans or a pie. My Grand-father, Buck used to say, "Always pay a little more than your share so nobody will think you're cheap."

Our hunting camp is a bit more elaborate than others. During the first week of deer season, we provide a few gour-met meals like steak, shrimp, or lobster. In Buck's day, they even hired a Dixieland band for opening weekend. But we can still count on my Dad, The Lion to belt out some old songs like "Sweet Gypsy Rose" and "Mack the Knife" on the piano. Those more adept at cooking usually take that role, while others do the dishes. There's usually a chance to target practice or shoot a bow and arrow. And there is the occasional cribbage or poker game with a few guys smok-ing cigars. If you wake up at 4 a.m. to go hunting or stay up until 2 a.m. drinking, then the afternoon nap time is pretty essential.

It has been several years since I have gone to camp during hunting season. The men-only tradition has been abandoned this year. The Lion, his girlfriend, their daughter, and three married couples his age are all spending opening weekend at the hunting camp. Hunting is low on their agenda. They are scouting out martinis and Bloody Marys. There is no shortage of time to drink and converse.

Gadget, my brother, has parked his RV camper on the lawn nearby to ensure he has privacy and a good night's sleep. He will be one of the few who are serious about hunting. He has shot a few big bucks...most of them were even legal. This year he douses himself with buck scent before heading out to his tree stand with wrap-around camouflage netting. Gadget hilariously describes this year's hunting camp as "senior citizens daycare." One woman has Alzheimer's disease. She intermittently breaks out in a song. She has not forgotten them. Her husband will patiently ask her to be quiet. During dinner she asks for the pepper. She does not use the pepper but places it in front of her plate.

I ask her, "Why did you want the pepper?"

She explains, "I find comfort in having it near me."

She also finds comfort in having her husband nearby. In the middle of the night, she yells out his name repeatedly until he wakes up and responds. He yells back, "I am right here! Be quiet and go back to sleep!"

The Lion has A.D.H.D. and sleeps with a radio tuned into a nostalgic country station that plays songs by Johnny Cash and Patsy Cline all night long. It's one reason that I sleep on the couch downstairs; besides, the bedroom loft is filled with a slew of drunken chatter, bodily noises, and a chorus of moans and groans. The Lion wakes up at around 3 a.m. and bangs around for an hour rearranging the living room furniture before he starts cooking breakfast.

I vow to be positive when I am around The Lion. As a son, I want to support him and spend time with him. But each day I need some time alone in the woods to keep my own peace of mind. I have not hunted deer for several years. I sold all my guns, but the thought of fresh venison on the table changes my mind. I purchase a license at the local convenience store and borrow my Grandfather Buck's rifle. I am going to go deer hunting this year.

COYOTE CRY NO MORE

It's unusually mild weather for November. The weather has been odd, and the apple trees did not bear this year. The deer are seeking alternative food, such as acorns. Early in the first morning of deer season, I climb up and sit in a tree stand. I have a nice view of the deer run coming from the maple clearing into a thick clump of pine trees on my right. After five minutes, a huge whitetail deer waves its flaggy tail and bounds out from the thick pine trees. I barely have time to swing my rifle in that direction. I can't tell if it is a buck or a doe. Now it has vanished up the mountain to safer terrain. But it gets my adrenalin pumping.

It's nice to just sit in the woods. I watch the chickadees sing, the squirrels scurrying about, and a woodpecker drumming on a dead log. I drink my ginger and licorice tea. Occasionally, I lift my gun to point it at tree trunks to make sure I can move quickly and quietly to shoot in all directions.

By mid-morning I prepare to leave. Suddenly, a young male coyote trots into the clearing near two bare apple trees. It's not aware that I am sitting so high above it in a tree. I raise my gun to look at it through the scope. I have spotted coyotes before while hunting nearby. I enjoy watching them with curiosity. I am not sure why I do it, but I take aim and pull the trigger. He is hit in the midsection. The coyote whimpers and cries out for a minute, scratching in the dirt with involuntary nerve impulses. I climb down the tree and walk over slowly with a feeling of great remorse. He takes his last breath beside a small pine tree. I start to cry as I pet his beautiful coat. I say to him, "I am sorry, you are so beautiful. I don't know why I shot you."

For me to kill this coyote is not normal. Perhaps I had a little buck fever and became trigger-happy. Being at camp and listening to hunters telling their deer stories might have brought it out. The coyote had always been a welcomed messenger. Swan Song even bought me a Native American necklace with a coyote howling. When coyotes howl, it reminds my heart of how Swan Song and I long to be together. They have a strong symbolic meaning to us. But coyotes are also known as tricksters. They deceive and mislead. That is certainly not what I desire before a potential union with Swan Song. Perhaps I felt this coyote was carrying a message that was unpleasant: something I did not want to hear. Whatever the coyote's message was, his death reminds me that life is fragile. This coyote will howl no more.

RETRIEVING THE RING

The senior citizens daycare and The Lion are set to leave on Monday. I stay alone at the camp for another day. The next day, I find a dead partridge mysteriously lying in the front yard. It is still warm. I pull the nicest tail feathers off and place the body in the woods for wild animals to eat.

Swan Song begins her Caring for the Heart counseling sessions today. I put a few logs in the box stove and settle in to pray during her sessions. I sing a few songs to set the mood. Then I pray aloud for her. I pray about the abandonment issues from her first marriage when her husband backed out on their wedding day. She often forgoes retelling the details. The short and sweet version she tells acquaintances is, "He left me standing at the altar."

I pray about her fear of authority figures and her desire to please other people. This probably relates back to her childhood. I can feel the Holy Spirit working with her to release some of the trauma she has experienced. Our hearts are so connected that I can sense her emotions. I can feel her pain. She has slight apprehension, but she is being brave. I hope that my prayers help create a safer space for her heart to heal.

The day before Swan Song and I plan to meet, I receive a message that UPS had made an attempt to deliver the package with the Desert Oasis engagement ring to my sister's home. Nobody was there to receive it.

I leave camp and urgently go to the UPS office. I ask, "Is there any way I can get my package today?"

They say, "The driver is in such a remote area that he can't get cell phone reception. But we can give you a few addresses close to your sister's home where the driver will deliver packages later this evening. You can intercept him en route and pick up your package."

I say, "Okay, let's do it!"

I hold my breath. Dusk is settling in. I wait patiently on the side of the road, near the driveway, at the appointed time. The UPS driver comes briskly up the road in his big brown truck. He stops in the road by the driveway, and hands the precious package to me. I feel a weight lift off my shoulders. I am so grateful. It all worked out. This must be God's plan. All along I had faith that it would. But I was not expecting it to be at the very last minute.

All week long I am filled with joy at the thought of proposing to my dearest beloved, Swan Song. We plan to meet tomorrow and then take a jaunt up to the rock ledge overlook at the top of Devil's Hill. It is here, at my favorite spot, where the view looks out towards Peacham Pond, Owl's Nest, and the rolling mountains in Peacham that I will propose to Swan Song.

Chapter 14

The Proposal

round noon, I meet Swan Song at the church. She has just completed her final Caring for the Heart counseling session.

I tenderly ask her, "How are you doing?"

She softly says, "I feel vulnerable."

"Are you up for a picnic?"

"Okay"

We drive down to Harvey's Lake to have a picnic lunch. Our conversation is kept light. It's nice to be with her again, especially on a gorgeous, sunny, fall day. After our picnic, I take a stick and write our names in the sand and place a heart above them. I am rather taken aback when she takes her foot and crosses out her name. It's not a good omen.

As we start to hike up the forest path, I bring up the topic of what a hero is. I start by saying, "A hero will express how he feels. It's an attitude. Like when I lift weights, I dig deeply because I want to be strong for myself and others."

I ask her, "What about you? How do you find your inspiration?"

She is breathing hard as she replies, "I am inspired by Kundalini Yoga. And I keep a disciplined diet."

She talks about an eleven-minute, forty-day journal practice that she created. She states, "My journal allows me to express my feelings in a continuous free-flowing style. At the end of the week, I read it and contemplate."

I notice that her foot is wrapped in medical tape.

Concerned, I ask, "Are you hurt?"

She says, "Nope. I'm good. It's a way to keep my feet in proper alignment. The medical tape keeps the bones in my feet from popping out."

I jokingly say, "Are you saying your body is held together with tape?"

She laughs and replies, "Yes, now that I'm older, tape basically holds me together."

We reach the summit, and I lead her to a small flat plateau area at the top of the rock ledges. The trees are mostly bare; the colorful fall maple leaves have all blown off. We look down upon the bare treetops. An island of pine trees distinctively stands out. I spread out a woven Mexican blanket. We take off our hiking boots and socks. It is a brisk fall day. We are grateful to feel the warmth of the sun in November. It shines upon us as we slowly smudge each other with sage.

I say, "I would like to put up some prayer flags for the four directions. Do you want to join me in saying prayers?"

She quietly replies, "Okay, but I want to say my prayers silently."

I unpack four long, cloth strips in the colors of red, yellow, black, and white. We make traditional Native American prayer flags by placing a quarter cup of tobacco on one end of the fabric. We pray as we wrap the end of each flag into a bundle. I say my prayers out loud. After each, she says hers quietly to herself.

I start my prayers, "Red is to honor a fresh beginning. Yellow is to bring healing. Black is to allow freedom and be grounded like a mountain. White represents purity, like the snow."

I ask her, "Will you sing that song to honor the directions, where you call in the grandmothers?"

She replies, "Sure." I love to hear her sing, as does almost everybody. With her beautiful, swan-like voice, she sings a Native melody that calls to the grandmothers from each direction. It asks them to come and be with us and give us their blessing. She kneels down to sit on her half of the blanket.

I creep barefoot along the rocks to tie four prayer flags on four surrounding pine trees. From where we sit, we can see the four strips of cloth hanging from each limb. Each is two-feet long with each color corresponding to its proper direction. White represents the north, red is for the east, yellow for the south, and black symbolizes the west.

I read two cards from a deck of affirmations by Louise Hay. The first says, "I am worth loving. I am willing to let love in. It's safe to let love in." The other says, "I release the past with ease and I trust the process of life. I do not use yesterday's mental garbage to create tomorrow's experiences. I create fresh new thoughts and a fresh new life." These seem promising!

Then I hand her two letters with cards inside. She had sent them to me in Virginia during the past few months. In one she had suggested that we go for a hike together in Vermont.

I enthusiastically say, "See, now we are doing it." In the other card is a picture of Krishna and Radha, the divine couple. Krishna is standing behind Radha in the garden, holding her as he plays the flute. Radha wears an orange, flowing veil, with glitter and jewels glued to the front of the card as her jewelry.

Swan Song had written in this card, "Thank you from my heart for holding me in all the ways that you do."

I awkwardly start into my daring proposal, "One of my dreams is to share my life with a woman who communicates openly, has her own life and friends, and is willing to work on herself." Swan Song listens intently.

I continue, "And it's you who has answered this prayer."

I compliment her on how much work she has done on herself, during this last season at Omega.

I playfully say, "Swan Song, close your eyes."

She replies, "Why?"

I tell her, "I have a gift that will express how I feel about you. But I need a minute to get it ready." She enjoys this kind of fun and squeezes her eyes shut. I have the large, white conch shell that I found when we were together on the beach in Costa Rica. It's bundled in a soft, yellow towel that is wrapped tightly with red fabric strips and topped with a huge, fancy, white bow.

I say, "No peeking, I am not ready yet."

She smiles and says, "I am keeping my eyes closed."

When her eyes are closed, I place the 18 partridge feathers I found at hunting camp in a circle around the huge white bow. They fan out to make a beautiful display with black and white zebra-striped feathers.

I softly say, "Now hold out your hands."

She holds out her hands. I gently place the wrapped bundle, with the feathers sticking out of the bow, in her hands. She opens her eyes and is delighted by the feathers. She smiles cheerfully like a child. She fumbles in her bag for her cell phone and takes a picture of it.

She carefully pulls out the feathers and with kindness asks, "Do you want to keep some?"

I wasn't expecting her to give any feathers back, so I say, "It's a gift for you, but if you insist, I will take three feathers."

She says, "I want to share them with you."

I pick out three feathers and she keeps the rest. Then she unwraps the red fabric strips from around the soft, yellow towel to reveal the conch shell. She knows how much I love it. She initially hesitates to take it.

She sighs and says, "I know how much this conch shell

means to you."

I smile and tell her, "I want you to have it."

She says, "Okay."

She accepts it and begins to unwind a spiraling web of baby blue ribbon that surrounds the conch shell. Tucked inside the conch shell opening is a two-inch square, thin, wooden box the size of a zippo lighter. It has the word LOVE carved on the center of one side of the box and a small heart inlaid in one corner on the opposite side. On the front of the box there is a secret sliding panel. Inside is the Desert Oasis engagement ring. It is placed gently on a piece of soft, yellow fabric.

She takes her time unwrapping the shell and holds the wooden box. As part of our gift-giving ritual, we flirtatiously take our time and embellish these moments.

I softly explain, "The box has a secret door."

I slide my finger on the box and edge open the sliding door. She continues to slide it open, and the Desert Oasis engagement ring is revealed.

She stares at it. She doesn't look at me but stares straight ahead. She becomes distant and her eyes glaze over. She is showing mild signs of shock. She is far away. It seems like she is catapulted back to the misery and grief from her past marriage. When I look at her face, I see only heartache, disgrace, and disappointment. This is not good. Her eyes proclaim, "Why is this happening to me?"

Still numb and disorientated, she slowly recovers to the present moment and vaguely says, "What kind of stone is this on the ring?"

It's pretty obvious what it is, but I say, "It's a diamond." Her mind is piecing it together. It seems like a part of her wants to deny what is actually happening. I feel some sadness about her reaction.

I look at her and softly say, "I am inviting you to share

our lives together. Please take this ring and take all the time you need to make a decision about marrying me." I take a deep breath and exhale. I expect it's going to take her a few months to decide.

Held Up by Love

Rare it is to hear pure Love tapping at my door.
I did not seek or invite it, but let us explore.
Could it be this love so pure chooses when and where to
  implore?
I peek through the eyehole and wonder who it could be.
I really must decide; do I dare open this door?
If I open the door, love will come in like a flood,
sweeping me off my feet, unpredictable, relentless,
barely giving time to breathe,
as I am turned and tossed in the waves.
Yet, in this slushy lushy love,
each moment is a present wrapped with a glistening bow
  and ribbon.
A gift offered to bring me closer to my own divinity.
What fool passes up such a gift?
Such a fool am I.
I dare not open that door.
Neigh, I did it once before,
the torrent of deceptive love,
smashed me against the shore.
But could it be this is a different man, a different time, and
  a different door?

NOT A LITTLE SURPRISE, BUT A BIG ONE

I don't expect an immediate decision. I am shocked when Swan Song turns to me sniveling and says, "I don't want to keep this ring. It's too valuable; you must keep it."

She turns and looks at me with tear-filled eyes and loudly says, "No. No. No. I am not ready to marry you."

I am too shocked to react. I am too numb to feel.

She pauses and says, "One of my worst fears is being asked to marry before we fully discuss it."

I apologetically say, "Given the situation, it did not seem appropriate; besides, I wanted to surprise you."

I hesitate and then ask, "Would you consider marrying me in the future?"

She pauses and says, "I don't want to say no, but I don't want to say yes because this may lead you to having false hope."

She continues, "I am not even ready to date you yet."

I am somewhat confused by her statement. When we were last at Omega, we spent most of our free time together. Sometimes we went to the movies or out for dinner. We have been on dozens of dates. We usually slept together in her tent. She came and spent three and a half weeks with me in Costa Rica. And now she is not ready to date me?

There is a long pause. We both look at each other and then out at the rolling mountains and the lakes.

I quietly say, "I will probably go to Costa Rica for the next year. It might be best if we have some time apart. I can visit you when I return."

She says, "I may be ready to date you in a year. We can go to the movies."

I perk up and say, "So there is some hope for us?"

She says, "I said I *may* date you; it's not definite."

I can't fully feel in this moment. I am not yet in touch with my emotions around her response. We spend time holding each other and more intense emotions surface. She cries again. I join her this time with tears streaming down my cheeks.

I softly ask her, "Are you a little surprised?"

She opens her eyes wide and says, "This is not a little surprise, it's a great big one!"

I remind her, "It will take me a few days before I can really get in touch with my feelings."

It's starting to get colder, and darkness descends as we walk back down the forest trail. She stops to admire layers of mushrooms growing sideways out of a tree.

I pop my head around the tree next to the fungi and, trying to lighten the mood, say, "Do you prefer this fungi to this fun guy?" We laugh. At least we can be ourselves even after being so emotionally vulnerable moments earlier. She gets cold and we stop. I rub my hands rapidly over her legs and arms to warm her. She warmly accepts my touch, as always. We laugh about how I move too fast in life, like a rabbit, and how she moves too slowly, like a turtle.

As we are walking down the trail, I say, "I am ready to live with you for the rest of my life, and you are ready to date me in a year!"

She reminds me, "I *may* be ready for a date in a year."

We start to drive back to her car. I hold her hand knowing it may be the last time we are together for a year. There is an awkward silence lurking in the air.

She says quietly, "I feel empty." There is nothing I can say. It seems like she is caught in a cold, dark place. I wish I could help her.

I stop driving and pull over to hold her for a moment. Then we continue. We pull into the parking lot where she left her car. On the car stereo, I play the song she had picked out as our song that summer. It's called, "I Won't Give Up On Us" by Jayson Mraz

At her car, she gives me a large poster of Krishna and Radha. It is a scene with the timeless lovers kneeling on a plush couch courting each other in the jungle. We hold each other and look up at the stars. I let her know that we can always look up and we will see the same stars. In this way, we can still be with each other. As she sits in her car, the streetlight mingles with the shadows on her face, and her silhouette reveals a gorgeous smile. This is what I choose to remember as we part.

Chapter 15

The Aftermath

I am lost in a fog for the next few days. I continue to sleep on The Lamb's floor on sofa cushions, but it no longer feels like I am making a grand sacrifice. I feel like a dog curling up with my wounded self-esteem. I try to get in touch with my feelings. My friend, Sunshine, suggests that I breathe into my heart and just feel, but this is too much for me to handle. I am afraid of feeling all the pain that will accompany Swan Song's rejection. I am free falling in a tail-spin, surrounded by dark, dismal clouds.

In Vermont, I visit a beautiful, stone Catholic church that one would expect to find tucked away in France. It sits atop a hill, amidst rolling fields, surrounded by gorgeous views of the green mountains. Swan Song and I once met here for a picnic in the flower gardens. I recall our lazy afternoon. We both sprawled comfortably on a blanket. My head rested in her lap. We had read Rumi poems to each other as we ate chunks of cheese and fresh strawberries. Now this is all in the past. I load my chanupa with kinnikinnick and securely set it in the Y of a tree branch.

Nearby is the Stepping Stone Spa. I walk over to take a sauna. During this same time, Swan Song is far away, participating in a sweat lodge ceremony. I sage myself and enter the sauna. In my mind, this will be my sweat lodge ceremony. I bring in my drum to chant and sing Native American songs. I do four rounds in the sauna. I raise the heat until it is unbearably hot. My heart and spirit are torn. I welcome the physical pain as relief. I better understand how My Native Brother felt during his eagle hang at the sun dance ceremony. I pray that Swan Song's heart will continue to be open and filled with love. I pray for my own healing. When I go into my heart, I do not feel pain; I feel only love towards Swan Song. I have a burning desire to be with her, as always. But I know it's not going to be that way for a long time. I console myself to keep going forward.

When I am finished in the sauna, I go back to retrieve the chanupa from the tree branch. The late afternoon sun is shining down as I walk through the grassy field by the stone church. The view through the valley looks out towards Willoughby Gap. I find comfort in gazing out at the two mountaintops. As a child, I imagined they were like two scoops of ice cream. They are no longer scoops of ice cream, but two mountains. We both grew up. I have fond memories of being with friends on the beach, hiking up the surrounding mountains, and biking along the shore.

As I stand surveying the view, my mind is drawn back to the last time I was there. It was with Swan Song just after she returned from Europe. We had our big talk on Devil's Rock. After that day, something shifted. I was never really the same. Before the deception, I had trusted her fully and completely. But on that day, I felt like she wanted to pull me into that dark, obscure place with her — into her deceptive web, with all her honey-coated lies. She has the power to rip apart my soul because I have given her the key to my heart.

It feels wrong. I love Swan Song and she loves me. She is far away with Chief Thunder Cloud — the man she told me she was leaving. It doesn't make sense. Why did she tell me she was available and unattached? Why did she come to Costa Rica? Why did we make love? Could it be she is afraid to let herself take the free fall that is required to really fall in love again after her heart has been broken. All I know for sure is that when we're together, we are both vibrantly alive. I also know Swan Song will not be in my life for the next year.

A refreshing breeze moves the grass in ripples across the field. I observe it dance and swirl. I let my sadness float away with the wind. After the sauna, I feel pure and ready to pray with the chanupa. I locate a spot at the breach of a hill and settle down on a woven blanket to gaze out at Willoughby Gap. Here I find the tranquility to say my prayers.

There is a life-size, snow-white statue of Jesus with both hands raised up toward heaven in front of the church. I go up and blow smoke from the chanupa on the statue of Jesus. After returning to my car, I notice that a quarter-size Australian opal containing lightning rainbow streaks has fallen off the stem of my chanupa pipe. It's starting to get dark. Somewhat distressed, I retrace my footsteps from the tree to the field where I sat, but I don't find the stone there. Then I walk to the statue of Jesus. I find the stone lying at his feet. I am so happy to find it that I hug the statue of Jesus.

During my overflowing joy, I whisper my deepest prayer to Him, "Jesus, please bring Swan Song back into my life."

I know I must go on. I must be a man about it. My thoughts are fuzzy and my whole purpose in life is unclear. My world has been shaken. I felt somewhere deep in Swan Song's heart, she wanted to be with me. I am the man she loves. We had an immediate connection the first moment we met. As our connection grew, I began to doubt if I ever truly loved anyone prior to her. Swan Song and I understand and connect with each other on so many levels. I sadly accept that she is not ready to join me.

Now I am much more aware of the harshness in the world. Before, I would notice the beauty; now I am drawn to the lack of beauty — the cold despair and desolation of being forsaken. It feels like I have been cast onto the dark side of the moon.

The best therapy I can find is scraping and salting the coyote skin behind The Lamb's senior housing apartment. When I am preparing the skin, somewhere in my mind I can hear the coyotes howling. At that moment, even a longing from our past is better than the empty, hollow feelings that reside in my heart.

I needed to know to what degree Swan Song was willing to stand up for our love. I have her answer. I must respect her decision, even though it's not what I want. Given her situation, the odds were probably not in my favor. I need not take her rejection as a personal attack on my self-esteem. I am still a worthy person. There is no need for me to get depressed or angry. She is not ready for marriage. She is not available for that kind of a relationship. She chose the most appropriate action to bring her what she felt would be the most happiness in her future.

If my actions were purely to meet my own needs, then I would be devastated. For me, the next level was to provide Swan Song with the beautiful experience of marriage — the way it's intended. If I expect Swan Song to try to please me or act in a certain way, I am constricting our relationship. I want us both to be free, even if that means we are not together.

An orange tree will naturally blossom and offer fruit. We may think this is our fruit tree and that it's intended to serve us. But if the fruit is not picked or lies on the ground uneaten, it's an offering gladly accepted by animals, birds, worms, ants, and the earth. My offering to share my life with Swan Song is not in vain. The orange tree is not attached to or trying to control the results. If I can learn to give like the orange tree, then I will be at peace.

RETURNING THE DESERT OASIS

My reality is that I am holding in my hand a very expensive engagement ring. I no longer have a car, and I have scraped the bottom of the barrel for cash. I humbly stay another few days with family and friends. I call and explain to Shellie, at Kokopelli Jewelers, the sad situation.

She empathetically says, "I can't believe she said no."

She knows I am in an emotionally tender place.

I reluctantly ask her, "Is returning the ring an option?"

By now, we have had numerous conversations. I remind her of a friend in Boston. Shellie speaks to the owner and he grants permission for my custom ring to be returned, minus 10% for their service and the shipping costs.

When I consider returning the ring, I start to cry. I went through so much to get it for Swan Song.

I tell Shelly, "I need time to make sure this is what I want to do." The ring captured what I wanted to express from my heart but could not with words. I am having trouble letting it go.

I call Swan Song and say, "I am considering returning the engagement ring. I need your help to make this decision. If there is any chance that one day you will wear this ring, then I need to know it now." Instead of answering on the phone, she writes me a letter.

Swan Song's Letter

The ceremony you created, the setting, the ring — all of it so beautiful and from the heart. Here now, I need to share my truth with you. Please hear my heart. The custom of surprising a woman with a ring is beautiful, romantic, and fabulous. But for me it's not complete if it comes before there has been in-depth discussions and agreement about a lifetime commitment together — that beautiful work of going into this consciously and together — every step of the way. In this way I have not understood this custom.

Working things through, together, in decisions that

concern us both is vital for me. Coming to a decision of marriage, for me, needs to take time and lots of life experience and talking and working through issues around things together. I just want your heart to be safe and cared for through this, since you went into such a vulnerable place with me. Even given everything I've been telling you, I need to be just friends with you right now.

You are so precious. You know what you mean to me, how I love you. This is really not about you at all. I want you to know how deeply you touched me. How amazing it was to be with you on that mountaintop, prayer flags waving, conch shell, love box, ring, and feathers. What devastates me is that it came at a time when I couldn't answer with a 'YES!' But yes is not the authentic response I can give in my situation. How devastating, not only to you, but to me. I hear you needed to do it for you. You wanted to let me know. For me: I am sorry this couldn't have come in a conversation and, if our lives moved us in this direction ever again, a big proposal would have come when we were both sure we were saying yes on every level.

Her responding letter did not remove all my reasonable doubt about returning the ring. Is she saying at a different time she might say yes? I need clarity before I make this big decision. Then I receive a text from her.

It reads, "If you need the money, then return the ring."

Her text has provided me with thirty minutes worth of courage. It is enough time to repack the ring and mail it back. I don't hesitate. There is a park in the center of my quaint Vermont town, with a bandstand in the center, surrounded by old maple trees. I somberly walk to the post office that is stationed at one corner of the park. I stand in front of the chest-high, gray counter surrounded by red and blue priority mailer envelopes. I gently place the glimmering, gold Desert Oasis diamond ring with the turquoise stones on either side, back into its original hard, ring case. I work slowly and mindfully, attempting to observe my movements.

My real feelings stay outside the post office. They hide somewhere behind a maple tree. The top and bottom of the ring case are perfectly covered on the inside with cream-colored silk cloth. I close it and place the case in a small cardboard box and seal it with packing tape. I surround this box with bubble wrap and place it, along with the appraisal letter declaring the value of the diamond, into a toaster-size box. I insure it and mail it back to the Kokopelli Jewelers. There is no need for rush delivery. Soon it will be cast back into the jewelry store case with all the other engagement rings. The ring is being given back, like a mother dropping off her unwanted baby at the adoption agency, with underlying hopes that somebody will give it the love and care it deserves.

I leave the post office and walk to the opposite side of the park where there is a quaint, old library. I am out of minutes on my cell phone and borrow The Lamb's cell to make another call to Shellie at Kokopelli Jewelers.

I stand in the middle of the park and say, "I have made my decision to return the ring." I spot my feelings peeking out from behind a maple tree. I motion with my finger for them to come get back inside my body. Like a disobedient child, they shake their heads and duck behind the tree. They listen in the distance like a child eavesdropping on a fearful grown-up conversation.

Not knowing the torment I have gone through to make my decision, Shellie asks, "Are you sure you want to return the ring? A woman can change her mind, you know!"

I speak slowly in a low growl, "Shelly, take the ring back."

Later, I receive a sympathy card from Shelly at Kokopelli along with a refund check for the ring.

She writes, "Words can't say how sorry I am to hear she said no. But hopefully sometime in the future she will change her mind and say yes!"

It seems my luck is running out along with my mom's cell phone minutes. The library is only open every other day. Today is one of those sunny but cold fall days, and it's just my luck that the library is closed. I balance my laptop on a wooden book-return box and use the library WiFi to make a Skype call to my Omega life coach, Nora Queesting.

She receives my call and says, "I am at the airport, waiting for my plane. We can talk until they start to board."

I bring her up to speed.

"I proposed to Swan Song and she said No... No... No... I just mailed the engagement ring back to the jewelry store."

She says, "Take a few breaths and feel what is going on inside your heart."

My feelings start to sneak around the corner of the library and they take a running leap and dive back into my body.

I quietly say, "I feel hurt and disconnected. I am a mess, completely undone. I want to cry, but it's too hard to do."

She acknowledges, "You took bold and courageous steps by expressing your feelings to Swan Song."

I rapidly say, "Swan Song said she is not ready for marriage. She said maybe she will *date* me in a year. We are still communicating, but she has left the state."

Nora gives me worthy advice, "Right now you need to focus on yourself and what you need. It's not productive to get caught up in thoughts about Swan Song."

I say, "Okay, I will try to take care of myself."

She asks, "What is it that you need right now?"

After a moment to get in touch, I say, "I find myself desperately wishing I could hug my dog, Thunder, in Costa Rica. That is what I need."

Chapter 16

Faith, Hope, and Love

With the ring refund, I purchase a one-way ticket for Costa Rica and leave the next Saturday morning. I rent an apartment in Heredia near where Thunder is located in a kennel. I need to settle down for a spell and pull myself together. I focus on improving my Spanish and getting in some quality walks, hugs, and play time with Thunder. I start to get in touch with what I really need. I join a local gym and regularly attend yoga, spinning, and Zumba classes. I need to stay grounded and remain flexible and strong in my body and mind. I lift weights a few times a week. Exercise helps clear my mind, and the Latino women in this gym are tough and beautiful distractions. To pass the time, I watch them do pushups and side planks. They lift one arm toward the sky in between rounds. I have no desire to be in a relationship, even with the gorgeous Latino women that surround me. There is currently no room for any other woman in my heart.

I push myself at the gym to physically and mentally get beyond what has happened between Swan Song and me. I try to keep myself busy. Being far away in a foreign country, my senses are hyper-alert, because I need to combat my loneliness. My feelings oscillate between extreme highs and extreme lows, with long, stable periods of the in-between. During all these times, I am nurturing a relationship with myself. But Swan Song captured my heart. I place her framed picture on a decorated corner stand in the kitchen.

Beside it, I keep a fresh red rose in a cup.

We agree to take a month without communicating to let ourselves process the marriage proposal. We call each other a few days before Christmas. I have let her know how I feel by proposing to her. I suggest that she initiates the conversations as we go forward, so it will be at her slow, turtle pace.

After two weeks, she wants to discuss the marriage proposal. I listen to her intently, then share my side. Every situation we go through is a process. Often we create false assumptions and don't understand each other's perspective or motivation until we talk about it afterwards.

She begins with an emotional waver in her voice, "A woman should not accept an engagement ring unless it's her intention to marry the man. I needed to make my decision on the spot!"

I say, "It seems contrary to your nature to make a rapid, on-the-spot decision about something as important as marriage. I can understand your reasoning, but I was counting on its being a process."

I sense that her emotions are somewhat frozen, but she has the genuine desire to work through it. She says, "I told you in the past I need to discuss marriage before it happens."

It did happen, but not to the degree she needed. I guess that is my fault. I was unaware that my marriage proposal would push her buttons.

I say, "Would you like me to explain the reasons why I proposed to you?"

She enthusiastically says, "Yes!"

I say, "It was the best way I could express how much I love you. I assumed that your Caring for the Heart counseling session would heal your past marriage issues. I was wrong."

She compassionately says, "We did work on my past

marriage and abandonment issues. But I need more sessions to resolve them completely."

Through our process, I learn to be more sensitive toward Swan Song. Through our conversations, I continue to listen and support what she needs to heal. Meanwhile, I continue to figure out what I need to do to take care of myself. I thought my future with Swan Song would be resolved and I would either marry her or my life would take a drastic turn without her. Neither has happened yet.

As a way to express my locked-up emotions, I create a one-hour video that guides me to laugh, cry, meditate, and worship. Through it, I am able to release many of my hurt and confused feelings. But I am still hanging onto a thread of hope, waiting to find out what will happen with Swan Song. She did say, "I *may* be ready to date you in a year."

FAITH, HOPE, AND LOVE

Around this time, the coyote skin I had nailed to the rafters to dry in a shed at Helen Keller's camp in Vermont has somehow wriggled back to life, jumped down, and run back into the woods. Before the proposal, it was my intention to send it to Swan Song, but now it feels awkward to offer her any gift after she has rejected the most precious one I could offer her: our life together. The coyote pelt vanished, like her affection, without leaving a track in the snow. I don't expect either will return.

Everything happens for a reason. I don't understand it all, but I do have faith in love. I want to write about love, yet Paul from the Bible has covered it rather elegantly. All we need to do is read it. The Bible guides me through the most intimate parts of my life.

"And now these three remain: faith, hope, and love. But the greatest of these is love. (1 Corinthians 13:13 NIV)

And we all know how Paul defines love?

"Love is patient. Love is kind. It does not want what belongs to others. It does not brag. It's not proud. It's not rude. It does not look out for its own interests. It does not easily become angry. It does not keep track of other people's wrongs. Love is not happy with evil. But it's full of joy when the truth is spoken. It always protects. It always trusts. It always hopes. It never gives up."

(1 Corinthians 13: 4-7 NIV)

This is amazing. My experience with Swan Song has led me down a long, winding spiritual path to discover the truth about love. Paul and I have learned much about love from Jesus. We both are sharing it in our own way. I am starting to understand... God is love. Love is in Jesus. Jesus is in me. I am love. Therefore, God and I are connected by love. God loves me and I love God.

This passage on love is worth reading twice. For fun I have included the Message version, which I slightly modified by adding the word (Love). If you want an additional perspective, after you read it once, replace the word "love" with "Jesus."

"So, no matter what I say, what I believe, and what I do, I'm bankrupt without love.
Love never gives up.
Love cares more for others than for self.
Love doesn't want what it doesn't have.
Love doesn't strut,
(Love) Doesn't have a swelled head,
(Love) Doesn't force itself on others,
(Love) Isn't always 'me first,'
(Love) Doesn't fly off the handle,

(Love) Doesn't keep score of the sins of others,
(Love) Doesn't revel when others grovel,
(Love) Takes pleasure in the flowering of truth,
(Love) Puts up with anything,
(Love) Trusts God always,
(Love) Always looks for the best,
(Love) Never looks back,
    but keeps going to the end."

(1 Corinthians 13:4-7 MSG)

I recall my last interaction with my life coach, Nora Queesting, at Omega. We decided to take a canoe from the beach back to her cottage. We talked casually about the situation with Swan Song. As we were pulling up to the shore, I desperately exclaimed, "I can't wait forever for her!"

Nora hopped out of the front of the boat and stood on the shore with her hands on her hips. I was still in the boat. She quickly refuted it by saying, "One of your options is you can wait forever!"

I paused, having never considered it before.

I took a deep breath and sighed. Then I said, "Yeah, you're right. One of my options is I can wait forever."

ONE YEAR LATER

This season I am a volunteer at the Abode of the Message, a Sufi community about one hour north of Omega. At the Abode there are no turtles near the pond, which I find unusual, but there are scores of rabbits. Swan Song and her turtle energy are nowhere to be found here. She makes plans to come visit one weekend a few weeks after my arrival, but changes her plans.

One month later, I go to our favorite camping site, which has a view of a marshy pond. There are four turtles sitting on a log. It might sound crazy, but to me it indicates that here is where Swan Song will appear. I make a campfire and fix my dinner. I call to let Swan Song know where I am and invite her to join me. She stops by that evening. We don't discuss any serious topics, but instead simply enjoy being together again as we sit in front of the fire. When it gets late, she drives back to Omega.

It has been almost a year since my marriage proposal. I recall her saying, "I *may* date you in a year." It is time to find out if she was serious about it.

I ask her, "Do you want to go out for dinner and a movie on my birthday?"

She replies enthusiastically, "Yes! I would love to." I am delighted and rather surprised that she said "Yes!"

The next day, she reads a prior email I sent her. I had written with a request that she tell Chief Thunder Cloud if we are going to be together, especially as a date. She texts me stating she has changed her mind. She no longer wants to go on a date. In her rollercoaster fashion, I get her answer.

SACRUM MELTDOWN III

I am not sure if my body can recover from a third sacrum meltdown. It has taken three to six months to recover after the first two, and the symptoms never completely go away. The first meltdown occurred when Swan Song ceased communication with me for the month after Costa Rica; the second was a year ago, after I left her at Omega.

A few weeks later, Swan Song and I plan to rendezvous again, for a second time, during a three-day weekend at our favorite camping spot. I have some anxiety about being together because, this time, I know we will have time to share our deeper feelings. Just prior to our meeting, Swan Song informs me that Chief Thunder Cloud and she are still partners, and her desire is for us to stay friends. I am still in love with Swan Song. This might be our final goodbye.

The day before our second meeting, I am working in an awkward position to drain the gas from the lawnmower at the Abode and pull the muscles in my lower back. One possibility is that these muscles are more vulnerable, but I know what is happening; my sacrum is having its third meltdown. I am anticipating our last goodbye. Initially, it's not as crippling as it was in the past. At least it didn't dislocate my sacrum and ribs this time. I tell Swan Song I won't be able to make it this weekend because I need time to heal my back.

That day I stay at the Abode in a retreat cabin doing stretches and breathing exercises for my back. I make an attempt to contact a friend, Izabella, to hang out, but I can't stop thinking about Swan Song. I can't even bring myself to take the steps to call Izabella, and I abort the attempt after a few tries.

LOVE VERSUS FEAR

I know my emotional attachment to Swan Song is unhealthy. I text Swan Song and ask if I can call in healing for us. She grants her permission. I pray to Jesus to come and heal our hearts. My heart is filled with frustration and resentment. I feel upset because my heart's desire is to be with her, but as long as the situation with Chief Thunder Cloud and her remains the same, I am in the same stale predicament.

That evening, I do a Caring for the Heart counseling session. I see a vision of my heart covered with snakes. Jesus comes and picks off the snakes to reveal a bright luminous heart. I can feel it burning and glowing. Then, he visits Swan Song's heart. I see a black, greasy sludge surrounding her heart. It's fear. I ask Jesus to provide her with some healing.

Love has no obligations nor expectations. With fear, we are expected to do things, and when our expectations are not met, it hurts. We may even blame others. If at a given moment one is living with more fear than love in their heart, then it's hard to respect anything, including yourself.

Jesus takes a fire hose and sprays the sludge off Swan Song's heart. It reveals a bright, glowing heart filled with love.

After my counseling session, I feel a shift. I am now able to call up Izabella. I leave a message inviting her to come visit me at the retreat cabin on the mountaintop at the Abode. This is a strong indication of a breakthrough.

Swan Song had once given me a quarter-size, red, transparent stone heart, which I carry in my medicine bag. I take it out and I take off the amber ring I first bought for myself when I arrived in Costa Rica. Buying the ring comforted me after being rejected from the marriage proposal. To symbolize letting go of any attachment to the situation with Swan Song, I take both items and toss them over the edge of a suspended wooden bridge that is known at the Abode as The Bridge to Nowhere. In the distance there are fireworks. It's a celebration. I am no longer as emotionally attached. I know it. I feel it. The best confirmation is when I return to my cabin. Izabella is sitting on the porch of the cabin. We chat while drinking tea and play a few songs from our cell phones. It is a comfortably pleasant evening.

Chapter 17

The Final Cut

DEFINING INTEGRITY

Late the next morning, Swan Song sends me a text. She writes, "I am at our camping spot starting a fire." I can't believe it. She still went there without me. I tell her, "My back is slightly better. I am coming."

Beloved
    "I slept but my heart was awake. Listen! My beloved is knocking:"
Lover
    "Open to me, my sister, my darling, my dove, my flawless one. My head is drenched with dew, my hair with the dampness of the night."
Beloved
    "I have taken off my robe — must I put it on again? I have washed my feet — must I soil them again? My beloved thrust his hand through the latch-opening; my heart began to pound for him. I arose to open for my beloved, and my hands dripped with myrrh, my fingers with flowing myrrh, on the handles of the bolt. I opened for my beloved, but my beloved had left; he was gone. My heart sank at his departure. I looked for him but did not find him. I called him but he did not answer. The watchmen found me as they made their rounds in the city. They beat me, they bruised me; they took away my cloak,

those watchmen of the walls! Daughters of Jerusalem, I charge you — if you find my beloved, what will you tell him? Tell him I am faint with love."

(Song of Songs 5:2-8 NIV)

I make the hour drive and meet Swan Song at our camping spot beside the pond. I arrive late in the afternoon and find her sitting cross-legged in front of the fire. She is wearing dark mala beads around her neck. She is in what she calls "stillness" and requests that I don't talk too much. She has just finished a weekend program immersed in shamanic teachings.

She enthusiastically tells me a little about it, "We, as humans, are evolving consciously at a rapid rate."

Eventually our discussion winds back to talking about our being friends. We both know we need clarity around what that means. I am not sure if I can handle being just friends. I am still feeling too much "in love" with her. Whenever we are together in private, we end up clinging together in an embrace. It provides boundless comfort. I am not sure if either of us wants to or has the ability to restrain that desire.

Suddenly, our conversation takes a feverish turn.

She confidently explains, "I am clear about my decision to continue in a partnership with Chief Thunder Cloud."

She repeats the word "integrity" again and again. It begins to feel like an argument.

She sighs and says, "I was in love with Chief Thunder Cloud in the beginning."

I cautiously ask, "Are you in love with him now?

She says quietly, "I would rather not answer that question."

She explains, "My decision to be in a relationship does not require being in love. My decision takes into consideration what will most benefit those in our community."

I cannot fathom being in a relationship for any reason other than love. She has a right to be in a relationship with whomever she chooses, for her own reasons. I will respect her decision, even though it breaks my heart.

We apologize for what felt like the start of an argument. She is sitting on a rock near a tree, watching the fire. I bend down on my knees next to her and bring my head close to hers. I understand her. In her list of life's priorities, our love is near the bottom. Our love is being washed away as no more than a forlorn illusion. I relinquish my dream of our being together. My hope has vanished. I feel dismal.

I lie down on a blanket by the fire. She massages my back, which is in pain from the drive and hauling all my gear to our campsite. Afterwards I massage her feet and hands. She loves to have her itty-bitty feet massaged.

She says, "I can't stay all night."

I quietly reply, "I understand."

Now, it's all about parting in a delicate way.

We cling together in my tent as we have always done, holding each other for the next three hours. I feel her restraining herself, trying to turn and pull away, not wanting to let her passion rise. Underneath, a part of her heart wants nothing more than to surrender to the moment. After a while, she falls asleep in my arms. I lie wide awake, holding her in the still of the night. I can feel her heartbeat near mine. I am aware that any sudden movement could nudge her awake and cause her to flee like a deer back into the darkness of the woods.

Being together feels different after nearly one year apart. My heart and hers have had some time to process and heal. We restrain from kissing. My lips were always elated to be near hers. They don't understand why hers are suddenly off-limits. This is where she has drawn her line. It is how she defines integrity. But I know the sad truth; *for integrity to truly exist, we must cease being together*. Lips or not, I am still drawn to her magnetically, but after tonight, I am no longer satisfied being physically intimate unless Swan Song is willing to tell Chief Thunder Cloud. I will no longer compromise the love and respect that I deserve. Nonetheless, my soul breathes a sigh. I have waited a year for this moment. All I have wanted in my heart was to hold her close again.

Part of me is relishing every moment and another part is regretting our inevitable parting. She softly stirs and awakes in my arms. Swan Song discreetly pulls herself away from our embrace and slips out of the tent. She stands by the fire, somber and sleepy. Her hair is disheveled. She vanishes silently into the darkness. She's not coming back. No matter how it happens, the final goodbye is always a dark night for the soul.

(This is the place in the story where I cry!)

DARK NIGHT OF THE SOUL

On a dark night, kindled in love with yearnings, – oh, happy chance! I went forth without being observed, my house being now at rest. In darkness and secure, by the secret ladder, disguised –oh happy chance!

In darkness and in concealment, my house being now at rest. In the happy night, in secret, when none saw me, nor I beheld aught, without light or guide, save that which burned in my heart. This light guided me more surely than the light of noonday. To the place where he (well I knew who!) was awaiting me –

A place where none appeared. Oh, night that guided me, Oh night more lovely than the dawn, Oh,

night that joined Beloved and Lover, Lover trans-
formed in the Beloved!

Upon my flowery breast, kept for himself alone,
there he stayed sleeping, and I caressed him. And the
fanning of the cedars made a breeze. The breeze blew
from the turret as I parted his locks; with his gentle
hand he wounded my neck. And caused all my senses
to be suspended.

I remained, lost in oblivion; my face reclined
on the Beloved. All ceased and I abandoned myself,
leaving my cares forgotten among the lilies.

— Saint John of the Cross

THE CAFÉ IN RED HOOK

We plan to meet briefly the next morning at JJ's café in Red Hook. I wait for her at a corner table by a window with my chamomile tea and a blueberry muffin. That morning, I had walked around in the forest for hours, recapping what she said the night before and all she has told me over the past three years. I am trying to fit together all the pieces in my mind. Perhaps my mind can comfort my heart, which is at a loss in this matter of love. I want to get closure and clarity for myself. I feel it will aid me to explain what I understand to be the current situation regarding her past marriage, her relationship with Chief Thunder Cloud and with me.

Swan Song arrives, but tells me she can only stay for fifteen minutes before she has to zip off to work. With this time limit in mind, I need to get to the point.

I rapidly say, "I want to tell you everything the way I see it, and if I am wrong about anything, please interject and correct me."

While I am talking, she stops me short to explain that our

commitment as friends has changed. She explains the new deal: "We will now heal ourselves and forget about sharing any of the messy emotional processes you go through." I am taken aback; our commitment as friends changed drastically. I am starting to feel a sudden chill. When did she decide this?

She adds, "And don't pray for me anymore." Ouch, that hurt!

I continue to quickly recap what I believe are the facts Swan Song has told me. I say, "Chief Thunder Cloud is your partner, but he has no desire to ever marry you."

She says, slightly irritated, "That is not true. There is a possibility that he could ask me to marry him. It has not happened, but it's possible."

I am flabbergasted. This is a big deal! I probably would not have proposed to Swan Song if I thought there was a chance that Chief Thunder Cloud had an inclination to marry her.

Swan Song stands up from the table and starts to shake her whole body up and down in jittery movements, like she is having a seizure. She couldn't care less about what anybody in the café is thinking.

She says in a jittery voice, "I need to release some energy."

She is getting anxious over our conversation, and her fifteen-minute time limit has nearly expired. I shorten our conversation to briefly touch upon the essential points.

Afterwards, she concludes with a breeze of a remark, "Your perspective of my life is a pinpoint of my reality." Then she gives me a slight smile, spins around, and departs. I watch her step out the door and walk down the street. Her wavy, dirty-blond hair is floating up and down. My eyes are soft. They still desire to savor her walking away.

FULL CIRCLE

I have come full circle. I am sitting in the café in Red Hook. It is the town where I first arrived to meet Pandora. My journey with Swan Song feels like it's nearing completion.

I begin to question Jesus, but He stops me in my tracks.

I am reminded of when Jesus asked, "If I asked, would you let go of Swan Song?"

After much turmoil I said, "Yes"

There is a higher purpose to all that has happened. It is surely beyond my own understanding.

I turn to the book *Jesus Calling* by Sarah Young. It reads,

> *"Trust me enough to let things happen without striving to predict and control. Relax and refresh yourself in the light of my everlasting love."*

My faith in Jesus is restored. He loves me and wants what is best for me.

After all I experienced around the marriage proposal, I came away with more integrity and higher standards for being in a relationship. Foremost, I know now how important it is to love and respect myself. If I allow our escapade to continue, then I am not doing so. I recognize and accept that her ways and mine were deceptive and disrespectful to Chief Thunder Cloud.

I have been told to never apologize for what I write. I need to break that rule. Chief Thunder Cloud was my friend. I apologize for how I deceived him. I am sorry for the pain and discomfort I caused due to my entanglement with Swan Song.

BURGER HILL

I leave the café and drive to Burger Hill. I return to the place I used to go with Swan Song. It seems like a lifetime ago when I kidnapped her to drum and sing, another time when we had healing ceremonies around her relationships, and again, a third time, as part of her woman's rites of passage.

It's a sunny fall day, and I stare out at the mountains to contemplate and absorb all that has occurred between Swan Song and me. I write a letter to Swan Song. I let her know our time together is complete. We have come full circle. I thank her for all her love, our fond memories, her sweet cards and gifts with pine branches on top, her smile, and the precious moments that we held each other close. Our connection is too precious and meaningful to erase my memories. I want to cherish them, so for now, I will continue to fondly wear the trade-bead necklace she gave me. I let her know that our spirits will meet again in another life, as we have done so many times before.

I roll the letter up as a scroll. When I returned the Desert Oasis ring, I also returned the small wooden box with the word "Love" carved in it, which I had purchased from a local jewelry store. There were too many emotions wrapped up in that box to keep it, but I did hold on to the small piece of soft, yellow fabric, which my mother had tenderly cut to wrap up the ring. I could handle keeping this small yellow piece, and I have carried it for the last year in my medicine bag, close to my heart. I take out the piece of soft, yellow fabric and use it to wrap around the center of her scroll to hold it tightly in place. I place the letter to rest in a protected hole in the heart of a big, old maple tree.

I am standing at the top of the knoll surrounded with rolling grassy fields with tall, bare, scraggly trees along the outer edge. It reminds me of a European landscape with trees formed by an artist's thin paintbrush. I am here to find my stillness. As I peer up, a bald eagle soars thirty feet overhead in the direction of the Hudson River. I can clearly see the details in the individual snowy white feathers that circle the neck and its tail feathers. I watch in awe, accepting this eagle as my confirmation to pray with the chanupa for Swan Song and Chief Thunder Cloud. I blessed them when their relationship began. I shall continue to send my blessing to Swan Song and the man she has chosen to be her partner: Chief Thunder Cloud.

The first time I saw a bald eagle in this area, I was on my way to the sweat lodge with Swan Song and My Native Brother, seven years ago. This eagle is another sign that we have come full circle. I step up on a flat granite stone with the surrounding mountaintops carved upon it and press the chanupa stem into my heart. I step in clockwise circles, chanting in a Native American language toward the surrounding valleys and mountains.

I feel tingling all over my body. It's the medicine man, Wichahcala, who Swan Song prayed to in her prior life as Wicahpi Ska (White Star) to be reunited with Cetan Luta (Red Hawk). He appears to me in a spiritual vision. Yes! It feels like I have come full circle. During this life, Swan Song and I were united in a way that brought us both healing. I hope the spirits of Wicahpi Ska and Cetan Luta are together. I am not sure. It feels like something is still keeping them apart.

He concludes by saying, "Iyuskinyan Wancinyanke-lo, Cetan Ohitika," which translates, "I am happy to have known you, Brave Hawk." "Toksha ake wacinyanktin kte-lo, I shall see you again."

I text Swan Song about the scroll and send a message, "I am at Burger Hill. A bald eagle just flew overhead. I am sending a blessing for you and Chief Thunder Cloud. I send you my endless love."

She responds kindly, "And my love eternal. I see you. You are ready to soar like that eagle. Be unfettered in every regard and spread your beautiful wings wide! You are a blessing in my life. I treasure the work we have done and are doing in this and other lifetimes. Thank you for the gift of you. May we always have each other's highest good a priority. I love you."

Chapter 18

The Shaman: Charcoal

EVICTION FROM THE HEART

Once a relationship ends, it's not really over. It takes time to get over the heartache. I will always feel love for Swan Song. Sometimes I get sucked back into believing that maybe, just maybe, our relationship could work out. This might be caused by soul ties that need to be energetically broken.

Thinking of her is less of an issue when I am busy in Costa Rica, but now after another winter, I have returned to the United States, and it feels like she is living inside my heart again. Lately I think of Swan Song when I am in a dreamy state, often before sleeping or upon awakening. Sometimes I feel like I am her. I like the feeling of light that radiates from her heart. When you get that close, your spirits merge. But I can't go on in this way forever.

If Swan Song lives in my heart, then she has a comfortable abode. I don't know if my heart really wants her to leave or if I can undo my cellular structure, which has relinquished itself to be devoted solely to her. It was a prerequisite I imposed upon myself prior to proposing marriage, given her past circumstances.

It's unclear if we can ever be just friends, but I am willing to try. I call up Althea, who led the healing class at Omega that cleared out all my past relationships. I am wondering if she can help me resolve this current one. I want to know if Swan Song and I can be friends; if not, I need help to remove her from my heart.

I tell her my situation. She says, "You need to call Swan Song and find out if she wants to be your friend: yes or no. Then ask her if she is open to the possibility of being in a relationship in the future. You need clarity, without a wishy-washy answer, to know how to proceed."

I say, "She is pretty good at being unclear with me because she does not want to hurt my feelings."

She says, "If she is unsure, then find out what it will take to give you a solid yes or no answer."

I say, "The last time we spoke, she told me that she is not available for a relationship and that Chief Thunder Cloud is her partner."

She retorts, "Swan Song is not in a *real* relationship with Chief Thunder Cloud. They just work together."

I say, "Yeah, I know."

She says, "You call Swan Song, find out the answers, then call me back."

My stomach starts to churn. Althea is direct and I need to know where I stand. I feel reluctant about calling Swan Song. When we texted a few days ago, she told me she was not wanting to communicate for two weeks.

I go for a walk up by the cornfield and stand under a shelter. It's raining lightly. Then it starts to come down in hard pellets. I am practicing what I want to say. Maybe I can just leave a message. Lightning strikes with a crack in the cornfield, followed by a huge *boom* of thunder.

I think back to my marriage day with Forevermore and how thunder spoke on that day. God's got my attention! He may be trying to say no matter what I do, Swan Song is a no go.

Then my cell rings. Hopefully it's God calling to explain. Nope! It's God using Althea to explain.

She says, "I only have a minute, I just spoke with Swan

Song. I told her that you were planning to call her and she became furious. I asked her if there was a possibility for a future relationship with you. She said no. I asked her if she wanted to be your friend and she said she had already explained her answer. It's no."

I say, "So it's clear. There is no possibility of a future relationship. She does not even want to be friends. Thank you. I know now what I need to do. I will evict her from my heart."

She says, "Did you say *evict*?"

I reply, "Yes I will *evict* her from my heart." Evict is the word that fits. It means force somebody to leave where they are staying when they are not willing to pay what is due.

I know what I must do. I need to make the final cut.

To seek some physical relief, I go to a local sports massage therapist. My muscles can barely budge. They are starting to become rigid and hard. I know the root cause is emotional. The massage therapist tells me about a shaman, Charcoal, and how she helped him. But, he says, he does not believe all the past-life stuff she told him. She said he was a murderer. He smirks with an evil grimace and says, "My massage is going to hurt you, but you will thank me for it later."

CHARCOAL: THE INVOCATION

I make an appointment with Charcoal. I am ready to have Swan Song removed from my heart. I buy Charcoal a gift at a garden store. It's a large, golden, clay sun with one eye that appears to be winking. There are gemstones in a circle around the outer edge. I have a strong feeling that Charcoal will remove Swan Song from my heart. My intuition says she can do it. Surely, this will warrant a nice gift.

I am led through a back room and up a set of stairs by a spry 71-year-old woman, no taller than my chest. She proudly lets me know that she just returned from hiking in the Sedona Mountains. It's renowned as a highly-spiritual place. I am glad she is feeling elevated. She will need to call forth some powerful energy to successfully perform this open-heart, spiritual surgery.

We enter her dimly-lit room. The smell of incense hangs thickly in the air. There is one huge altar table with a large, white porcelain statue of Buddha cupping a blue glass marble in folded hands that rest upon his lap. I am glad to see a glittering card of Jesus standing at the front of her altar near the pillar candles. The whole room is carefully decorated with an array of spiritual paraphernalia. I am sure many were personal gifts from other clients. Each one, like my gift, has a meaning that is relevant to her.

She sits me down in a swiveling, banana-shaped chair covered with a sheet, and places a pillow behind my neck.

I look surprised and ask, "Is this where I will be when you perform my treatment?"

She asks, "Are you here for a reflexology session?"

I sigh and reply "No! I am not sure you can help me."

I explain the trauma in my sacrum that was caused by my last relationship.

I softly say, "She is still in my heart. I want her removed."

She confidently says, "I can do a Reiki session from head to toe, but it's God who will do the healing. The Arch Angel Michael will come with his blue sword of light and slash away."

I enthusiastically say, "Now, that is why I am here."

She has the kind look in her eyes of a grandmother; behind her spectacles is a small, square face framed by her shoulder-length, bark-colored hair. She directs me from the banana chair to sit down in a large armchair.

She takes sage oil and pours some on my palms.

She instructs, "Rub this oil around in a circle and then

inhale it deeply three times. Then I will rub a little frankincense oil on your back."

Afterwards, she sits down in a chair beside me. She says, "We will start with a meditation. Let's begin with three Om's."

She leads by saying "Om" and I follow, but fail in my attempt to match her tone. During the second Om, I start off low but adjust to synchronize with her. On the third Om, she changes the tone in the middle and brings it up to hit an extremely high note. I join her in the tone shift. It feels like we just went down a slide on the playground.

I am sitting there meditating with my eyes closed while she starts her invocation.

She says with vigor, "I call on the Arch Angel Michael with his blue sword of light and a band of one thousand angels, Jesus and the Holy Spirit, Mother Mary, Father Sky, Mother Earth, the directions of the north, south, east, and west..."

When she is done with her rather lengthy invocation, she invites me to sit on the edge of the massage table.

She refers back to the toning, "Now wasn't that Om fun?" It was fun, but I am acting rather somber because I am here for a serious spiritual removal.

She says, "You had fun doing it. Don't you dare tell me you did not!"

I lighten up some. She lights sage and smudges me with a long turkey feather.

She says, "This sage came from South Dakota, and I only use the purest oils."

Of course, the scent of sage immediately reminds me of Swan Song and the way she would smudge herself every evening upon returning to her tent. I am feeling more comfortable. I lie on my back on her massage table as she covers me with a sheet and places a handkerchief over my eyes.

THE REIKI TREATMENT

She places an amethyst stone beneath the massage table under my crown chakra, a rose quartz stone under my heart, and a smoky quartz stone under my feet. I feel the channels in my head and feet open with a tingling sensation.

She says, "The sages and saints, healers and prophets that are working for the divine light of God are here in this room."

I can sense Althea in the room, or at the very least, her intentions and prayers for my healing are present.

Charcoal places her hands on my forehead, and I feel the heat coming through. I was not a big believer in Reiki because I never had great results with it. But today, the time is ripe. God uses Reiki as His chosen channel for my healing. It's the laying-on of hands. Thoughts of Swan Song start flashing through my mind. They are being pulled out and away in long strands. I feel the space where the grooves of her thoughts existed being filled and smoothed over with light.

I tell Charcoal, "They are working on my thoughts."

She says, "Be open to it. Twitching and yawning are signs that you are releasing. Do what you need to release the energy. Don't hold back."

Once she is done by my head, she claps her hands together, then moves on to the next spot by my neck. In my vision, I see Swan Song standing in my heart.

I ask Charcoal, "Do you want to know the name of the woman?"

She replies, "Oh Yes! What is her name?"

I feel emotions swell up as I speak, "It is...Swan Song."

Swan Song has set up camp in my heart. It's somewhat like her tent. She has made herself comfortable along with all her belongings. I need not evict her; she knows that she must go. There is no sense of urgency in her actions; she calmly starts to pack her bags. There are boxes of books, clothes, and bedding. It all goes into baskets or containers, as if she were leaving Omega at the end of the season. I often assisted her in the real world by carrying her bags and baskets to the parking lot during her weekend escapades.

In my vision, she says, "I need help carrying my bags."

I say, "I cannot help you today. There are lots of angel and light workers around; why don't you ask if they can help move your bags?"

She smiles and they willingly comply.

Lastly, her tent and bed are dismantled and hauled away. Swan Song is just standing on the empty tent platform.

I am reliving the moment along with her. We take time to absorb and release our seasons of fond memories. It's as if our past times together are being played backwards, like a movie on rewind. I twitch as I view my proposal to her on the top of Devil's Hill. Then our favorite camp spot by the pond. How we cherished our time beside that campfire. The way I held her body close to mine under my buffalo robe. Then our endless encounters at Omega. Dancing in the moonlight, her smile, the joy she radiates, the way I felt so fresh and alive in her presence. The days we spent on Burger Hill drumming and singing. And earlier when I was with her, Lost Son, and Feather Maker in her big tent. Then our first visit at my retreat space with Pandora, but instead of her coming in and giving me flowers, I hand them back to her, and she walks out the door backwards. My memories and the feelings I relate to Swan Song are being drawn out and flushed away.

She stands there on the platform alone, no regrets. She is pure and divine in her beauty, fully acknowledging and appreciating our love and friendship for all of its goodness. Charcoal claps her hands to signify that she has finished on my neck. As she begins to lower her hands down towards my heart, Swan Song fades away and disappears. I am fully present for it.

PAST LIFE KARMA

My vision of the healing does not end with Swan Song's departure, but it moves on to our past lives. The first is when we were children, as a brother and sister, trapped under a school building in India. The feelings become overwhelming. There is a part of my karma that I must release. Its dark; Swan Song and I are both trapped down low but able to crawl around. We touch each other's hands. She is the first to die. I cannot bear to go on living without her. With her death, all my hope diminishes. What I want more than life is to be with her. I choose death over life without her. This is my karmic burden. I burst out in uncontrollable tears on the table. Charcoal senses my feeling of being crushed and gives encouragement.

She says, "Keep open. Let it release. Breathe through it."

I am feeling huge shifts in my torso and continue to twitch and release. Charcoal finishes at my heart and claps. She is doing a lot of blowing and whishing away. As she progresses down my body, there is a flow of relaxation in the muscles in my chest and shoulders. When she proceeds below my heart, in my intestinal area, it feels like the corpse of a dead animal is being pulled out from my insides. As Charcoal moves toward my sacrum area, I sense we are approaching the past life we shared as Cetan Luta (Red Hawk) and Wicahpi Ska (White Star).

I politely make a request to Charcoal, "Can you smudge with sage near my sacrum?" She quickly lights up more sage and smudges my backside.

During this past life, I only see blurry glimpses in my vision, but I feel intense emotions. My past lives are still in reverse. She creates a cloud of smoke that hovers above my body as the sage is poured on thickly. Wicahpi Ska is having to console our kids about my death. I feel her anguish. She wants to be a strong mother, but she, herself, is torn up inside. I know the next thing I am going to feel is the grizzly bear's claws like a knife jabbing into my back. I am bawling like a baby on the table. It's overwhelming! The tears are running down the sides of my face. I feel the moisture of the tears gather in my left ear. I can't fully see what is happening other than a swirl of sunlight and green branches. I'm in a seamless place. Time continues to travel backwards in slow motion. Cetan Luta and Wicahpi Ska are together before he died.

At that precise moment, Charcoal yells out, "Call back your soul! You need to get your soul to come back! Do it now! Call back your soul!"

There is a lot going on. I don't think Charcoal understands everything that is happening. And this is not the right time to explain. It's not my soul that is reuniting; it's theirs. Somehow their souls were still kept apart, even after all we have been through. Maybe this is how it all had to happen. But I know at this moment, without any doubt, their souls are reunited.

Charcoal says, "Roll over on your stomach."

She continues near my sacrum, as if the other half of the corpse of that dead animal in my intestine is now being tugged out my tailbone. I hug a pillow under my chest and continue to cry face down. But I am no longer crying over the intense emotions from the bear attack or Wicahpi Ska's sadness. Now my tears are feeling ecstatic joy for Cetan Luta and Wicahpi Ska being together.

Charcoal says, "Just keep letting it go."

The world I know is clashing around; my mind is frantically trying to figure it all out. I thought I was Cetan Luta in my past life. Yes! I had just felt the bear's claws. Our spirits are definitely separate now, and he has just reunited somewhere in the Spirit World with Wicahpi Ska. This must mean that Swan Song's spirit is also separate from Wicahpi Ska. But didn't we both live as them? I feel my soul is fully back in my body. But it is, or was, him, or a part of him. His spirit worked through me in this life to fulfill what it needed to do in the spirit realm.

Now they are together in the Spirit World, but Swan Song and I are apart in this physical world. I believe we came together as them in this physical plane because they couldn't do it in the spiritual one. That part makes sense, but I still feel confused. Why can't Swan Song and I be together? It's simply complex.

WICAHCALA'S BLESSING

Charcoal places her palms on the bottom of my feet, and my body fills with golden light. She stands up near my head and starts to chant in a Native language. I just listen to the words and let them do what they need to do. This is no normal Reiki session. It feels like Charcoal's chanting is channeling through to the medicine man, Wicahcala, who just slipped in the backdoor.

He is present to give us all his final blessing. Now that the spirits of Cetan Luta and Wicahpi Ska are reunited, his commitment to Wicahpi Ska is complete. The circle is full. Maybe he knew I could not bear to live with Swan Song in my heart. The guidance and shamanic healing provided by Charcoal and Althea and the medicine man, Wicahcala, were all orchestrated with precision. It removed Swan Song from my heart, cut our primary past karmic bonds and reunited their spirits. We are all connected to the circle: past lives, and present lives, spirits and those in the flesh. We are here to help each other. Sometimes we get to receive; other times we must give. In my case, I had to give up and let go of Swan Song completely.

After the session, Charcoal admits, "Yes, it turned into a shamanic healing, but most people around here are not open to that."

I say, "I am fine with it."

She confesses, "More entities came out of your body than anyone I have ever worked on."

Charcoal leaves me alone in the room for ten minutes. When she returns, she cuts the energy cords to close our session. It feels, after this session, that Swan Song and I have severed our soul ties. I am free at last.

For now, I stand alone. Swan Song is neither by my side nor living in my heart. I feel as whole and complete as I can. Swan Song is on her own journey. She is always a reminder that there are still a few remnants of magic left in this world.

"When a man or woman on a spiritual path faces adversities, they will not seek refuge in a friend who provides comfort by encouraging their fruitless ways. How much better to find a friend who will unwaveringly aid them to courageously endure their suffering and pass through it. When repeatedly exposed to such vulnerability, the psyche will eventually dissolve, revealing their indestructible divine inner glow."

Afterword
Acknowledgements

I would like to thank all my friends and the professional editors...Nick, Nicole, and Claire...who edited my book. Natalie did a fabulous job resurrecting the Swan Song section. (She assisted by pulling out of me those emotionally crucial parts that I wanted to avoid.) Lost Son taught me about flow and non-judgmental writing and added his personal contributions. A special thanks to Joan W. and Janet, who both provided valuable editing assistance. Vi Waln (who was an editor for the Lakota Country Times) and Swan Song reviewed parts of the Native American section.

A special thanks to Wayne Scott of Swan Lake First Reserve of Manitoba, Canada for his poem: SunDancer. All the major characters (whom I could locate) were sent the sections about themselves to review. I appreciated the feedback from Swan Song, The Lion, The Lamb, Pandora, and Lost Son.

My mom, The Lamb, as always, went far above the call of duty. She was there to offer her support, editing skills, assisted with research, improved my grammar, and kept me honest. Lastly, to all my friends and family who read the book, I love you.

Just for Laughs

Editors' murmurings
and correspondence

"You need to write, knowing Swan Song will never speak to you again."
— Natalie

"I definitely cannot tell you how many beers I had on any given evening a decade ago, but I can tell you what I know about myself from living with myself for 54 years…assuming I was at my worst, my best guess would be that I may have had up to 7-9 beers that night, as I don't recall ever having more than 9 beers over a 3-4 hour period at any time in my life."
— Lost Son

"I read over Swan Song a few nights ago. Then I cried for all you have been through. I love you."
— Mom

"Change my name, you are not going to call me Lolita."
— Pandora

RESOURCES:

The Author, Randolph C. Phelps,
P.O. Box 255, Danville, VT 05828

Cristo Morpho Inc.,
E-mail: cristomorpho@gmail.com
Web Site: www.cristomorpho.com
Facebook: Cristo Morpho Community

HEALERS:

Don Candido Morales, Indigenous Plant Medicine, Costa
Rica Email: candido.centroculturalindigena@gmail.com
Facebook: Candido Culture Indigena 011 506 2756 8127
www.onehumantribe.com "The Hidden People"

Althea (Elaine Koelmel), Meditation Teacher, Sarasota, FL
Email: illum.innate@verizon.net

Caring for the Heart Counseling Ministry,
Colorado Springs, CO
Email: caringfortheheart@msn.com (719) 572 5550
Website: www.Carefortheheart.com

Life Coach, Nora Queesting (Suzanne "Mileka" Damberg)
New Lebanon, NY
Email: youdeserveacoach@yahoo.com (917) 656 4637

SPIRITUAL RETREATS:

Omega Institute
150 Lake Dr.
Rhinebeck, NY 12572
www.eomega.org
(845) 266-4444

Abode of the Message
5 Abode Rd.
New Lebanon, NY 12125
www.theabode.org
(518) 794-8090
Saluk Academy www.sulukacademy.org

Satchidananda Ashram (Yogaville)
108 Yogaville Way
Buckingham, VA 23921
www.yogaville.org
(800) 858-9642

Bibliography

(1) Gems, E. (2010). *Native American medicine wheel: What is medicine.* Urbana, OH www.crystal-cure.com. Permission granted by Emily Gems. https://crystal-cure. com/article-medicine-wheel.html

(2) Lim, E. (2015) AkashicSecrets.com Akashic Records information shared by Evelyn Lim, Intuitive Consultant, Singapore. Permission granted. http://www.akashicsecrets. com/akashic-records/

(3) Gems, E. (2010). *Native American medicine wheel: What is the significance of the medicine wheel?* Urbana, OH www.crystal-cure.com Permission granted by Emily Gems. https://crystal-cure.com/article-medicine-wheel.html

(4) National Library of Medicine. (2008). *The medicine wheel and the four directions.* Bethesda, MD: U.S. National Library of Medicine. Open source: https://www.nlm.nih. gov/nativevoices/exhibition/healing-ways/medicine-ways/ medicine-wheel.html

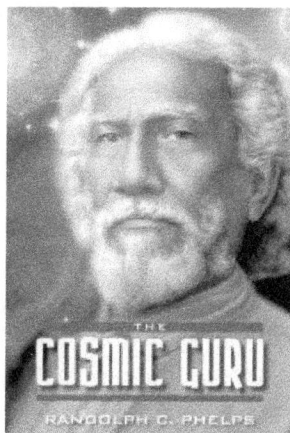

The Cosmic Guru

While in an advanced inverted yogic posture, I feel a tingling sensation throughout my body. Then I hear the voice and feel the presence of Swami Sri Yukteswar, a guru of wisdom, who claims to have entered my body. I've acquired some new spiritual gifts, including the ability to speak 50 languages. For the next 10 days, I am sky-high in a spiritually-altered state. Pastor R.I.P., John Wayne, a spiritual dowser, and Frenzy, my acupuncturist, all want to perform their version of an exorcism to get this Guru, which I am enjoying, out of my body. I attempt to figure out the truth, while facing some of my deepest fears. Along the way, false impressions arise through all of my senses, leading me to discover I can't rely on what I have always trusted...

After my Guru experience, I begin a passionate 10-year quest to find God, Truth, and Love. I plunge into an eclectic yoga practice; experience soul-stirring, guided Sufi retreats; and embrace two Lakota Sioux traditions, the Sweat Lodge and the Peace Pipe. I try to understand Jesus, amidst unsettling friction with my church pastors. In time, the love of

Jesus pours out through all my brokenness.

"Reading your chapters made me weep... They were flowing like honey... I could just picture Jesus talking to you."

— Nina B, Christian Prophetic Artist

The *Cosmic Guru* includes the final guided meditation where the reader is guided to receive a word of wisdom, a vision, or healing. The meditation is intended for those who have read *Swan Song* and *The Cosmic Guru* or *Ten Minutes, Ten Days, Ten Years*.

SAMPLE FROM THE COSMIC GURU

Two police cruisers slip silently down the middle of the long dirt driveway toward my family's three-story brick home. Pine trees, 100 feet tall, are staggered along either side of the driveway as if javelins were thrown down from heaven, just missing these intruders. I peer out to see them through a small side window beside our white front door.

I run upstairs, out of breath, and enter my sister's bedroom. Vinyl wallpaper covered with foot-long red roses surrounds me on all sides, but this situation does not smell sweet. Panicked, I open the second story window that faces the river.

In the distance, under a cluster of pine trees, is a granite platform covered with pine needles. A prior owner in the late 1800s built it as his throne. I imagine him sitting like a dignified statue gazing down upon the waterfall while he contemplated life's intricate ways.

If I could jump out far enough, I could grab a branch of the giant pine tree near the house. I squat like a bird on the window ledge, pausing to ask myself, "Is this the right moment to allow The Guru to have full control of my body?" It seems like a reasonable solution and an easy way to escape this predicament, but deep down my soul suspects that to surrender itself to another spirit is breaking some sacred spiritual ethic. But then again, why not?

Ten minutes earlier, I was sitting in the lotus position on top of a four-foot-long, gold-framed antique mirror that I had taken down from the bathroom wall and positioned on the edges of the tub. It felt as though The Guru sharing my body for the past ten days was ready to blast out of my third eye. I had positioned the Waterpik shower-massager to direct a strong half-inch beam of water toward my third eye, which I was intently focusing upon. I became distracted by anticipating a jolt as The Guru departed, and I was suddenly overcome by fear. I envisioned a sudden blow of pain that might throw me into the shower wall with tremendous force. I found myself beginning to scream as long and loudly as is humanly possible in one breath. Although this eased my fears of imminent bodily harm, it didn't occur to me that my screaming would raise the concern of my mother, who immediately called the police.

Perching on the windowsill with my heart beating rapidly, I make my plea. "Guru, take over complete control and get me out of this situation!"

What happens next is hard to explain. It's as though I am looking through a periscope. I can't see anything to the left or right unless I turn and face that direction. Jumping to the tree branch seems more challenging now, but begins to look more realistic when it comes into focus through my tunnel vision. I leap from the window ledge and catch hold of the branch.

Life is looking better, I fantasize about taking a nice easy float down to the soft, pine needle-bedding … but before this happens, I hear a crack! and a snap! My descent suddenly turns into a crash landing. My ankles feel slightly sprained, but they still function. Deciding to run, I discover it's not that easy with tunnel vision. I see a foot here, a branch there ... look out for that tree! I make a quick left turn. There's a steep, fifty-foot descent to the river. I find myself airborne, somewhere near the granite platform, floating or flying, a big rock heading my way. I feel the impact, hard against my skull. Blood trickles down my cheek. I feel numb, sick, and woozy.

Time passes: ten minutes ... ten days ... or ten years? As if in a dream, I stand up and wade through the waist-high ferns. I feel like a cornered warrior, forced to retaliate.

I come back to something resembling reality when a tranquilizer is injected into my hip. This wakes me up from one dream and puts me into another. I first notice the smell of hot vinyl seats. Then I realize that I am locked in the back of a police car and have pepper spray in my eyes and a black mesh sack over my head. I feel blood on my face and hands, and my ribs feel cracked or broken. It's painful to breathe. My right shoulder has a bloody scrape where I was dragged on the ground. I feel chains on my lap that lead to a set of handcuffs around my wrists and a pair of ankle cuffs below. I have been captured like a prisoner.

But this is not fiction. These events are real. What happened during those ten minutes after I crashed into the rock until I was brought back to reality in the police car? I reveal the unusual events during the ten days preceding this scene, and the amazing spiritual journey that unfolded during the ten years thereafter. ■

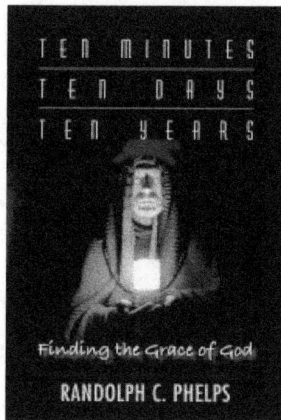

Ten Minutes, Ten Days, Ten Years: Finding the Grace of God

This is a brilliant melding of three intriguing stories. It will fill your soul with joy and substantial inner courage. Each character is given a fun, revealing pseudonym. Over a span of years, their insights and behaviors reveal a steady advance toward spiritual maturity. You learn how their lies and deceptive ways are uncovered and the merits of cultivating intimacy and integrity. Along the path, you discover how they face the challenges of personal addictions, triangle relationships, and emotional anguish.

"This book took me on a ride though different metaphysical planes, past lives, and dimensions."

— Natalie Nichols

This book is a compilation that includes *The Cosmic*

Guru and *Swan Song*. It includes the final guided meditation where the reader is guided to receive a word of wisdom, a vision, or healing.

Wise Wolf on Retreat

It's the break of day at the top of the mountain. I walk slowly along the forest trail. I am observing the great oaks and the mostly-bare maple trees and how they are spaced apart symmetrically, like soldiers dressed in camouflage. A gray squirrel and a few blue jays are in the tree branches, part of the costume worn by the forest. I feel that the trees can sense my footsteps as I tread on the chestnut earth beneath them.

I inhale and take a step. With my exhale, I take the next step. I feel my heel and toe touch the earth. My steps are like whispers. I am still enough to hear my heart beat four times between each step: *thump...thump...thump...thump.* The orange sunrays peek through the leaves, and a few golden beams spotlight down upon overzealous grass patches. The shadows near the tree trunks show a dark contrast, and broken twigs lie randomly scattered about. I can smell the moss draped on the northern side of each tree. I slowly step forward on the path out into the rays of sunlight. It shines on my hands and cheeks. I pause to feel the warmth and welcome it on my skin.

In the distance, I hear the gentle, deep tone from a set of wind chimes. *Ding...dong. Ding...dong.* There is a gigantic set of chimes dangling on top of the retreat mountain. They are here to represent the elements of the wind. I see the four shining, silver bars, like elephants' tusks, hanging down from forty feet above, where they are tied to a branch of a giant oak.

I slowly, step by step, make my way to the giant chimes. I stand underneath them and slowly gaze up. The gigantic chimes are suspended directly above me. The sound reverberates through my cells. When I move slightly to the right or left, the perfectly resounding tone is distorted. I remain still in my chamber. The energetic tone is thick, like warm chocolate being poured on my head. I feel it drip down my arms and chest before it forms a small puddle around my feet. I am tempted to stoop down and take a lick. But I remain still.

I look down another trail. There is the silhouette of a man walking in my direction. As he comes closer, I can distinguish that he is wearing slightly weathered jeans, leather work boots, and a blue sweatshirt with the hood over his head. The cloth veil over his face glistens. It is tucked in under his hoodie to cover his face. But I know him by his walk. One hip is tighter and slightly pulls out. His short steps, combined with his white beard behind that veil, resemble that of a wizard. He is my mentor, Wise Wolf. I am glad to see him here. He is on the mountain as a participant in his own ten-day retreat.

As he approaches, I smile and expect him to acknowledge me. He knows I am here. It is obvious. I hold back the urge to give him a big bear-hug. That is how he usually greets me. Yet, Wise Wolf peers straight ahead; he is focusing intensely within. Perhaps this walk in his heart is melting the trauma and stressful hours he spends as a hospice worker. His retreat time is precious. He holds every drop of energy compassionately. He continues to deliberately step forward, as if a cement statue has broken free from the mold to take its first few slow, silent steps. There is not so much as a nod as he walks past. I am mesmerized by his slow, mime movements. Or is it the inward concentration?

I reminisce about our past mentor meetings; how he would sit on the edge of a chair, listening intently. Once he said firmly, "Why are you beating around the bush? If you have something to say to me, just say it!" He was right. After that day I did. He was the first man older than myself that didn't scare the crap out of me. I felt he trusted me, and I trusted him. I was comfortable enough to talk about anything with him. This meant a lot. It was a breakthrough, because both The Lion and Pastor R.I.P. had instilled the belief that they would not trust me.

Wise Wolf was there to listen during my darkest moments. I confided in him that I sometimes had mixed feelings about being on a spiritual path that involves yoga, Native American traditions, and Jesus. I find that many Christians are offended by my involvement in Native American traditions or yoga. They expect me to follow Jesus, exclusively.

Wise Wolf said, "All these paths come together within you."

I desire to obey the Holy Spirit. When I participate in yoga or Native American traditions, Jesus and the Holy Spirit are right beside me. If I am not sharing them as part of my truth, then I am offending myself. The Holy Spirit wants me to be myself. Some people may not be pleased with my not following Jesus, exclusively. It is not my role to make them happy. Regardless of what others think, I need to respect and love myself, every day. The real question is: *Can they love me for who I am?*

About The Author

Randolph C. Phelps is a native Vermonter and a resident of Costa Rica. He is the founder of the Vermont non-profit, Cristo Morpho, which established a sustainable, spiritual community located on the Caribbean side of Costa Rica, called The Cristo Morpho Community. During winters, he hosts visitors and directs the Cristo Morpho Volunteer Program, which focuses on immersion into the community through individual service projects, and fostering spiritual growth.

Randolph was a wedding and stock photographer, traveling to Alaska and Australia to photograph the natives and wildlife. His photographs have been published in magazines such as Faces, Challenges, and vacation guides for Alaska Tourism Council and brochures for The Experiment in International Living. His poems have been published in the Green Mountain Trading Post and in the book *Nothing hardly ever happens in Colbyville, Vermont* by Peter Miller.

Randolph has a B.A. in Business Management and was enrolled for a Masters degree at Saint Michael's College in Colchester, VT. This included one semester abroad at Melbourne University to study Australian culture. He is certified by the American Sailing Association for Basic Coastal Cruising. He is a certified Integrative Yoga Therapist specializing in chronic conditions and restorative postures, an Integral Yoga Teacher, and a Thai-Yoga bodyworker. He is also trained as a "Caring for the Heart" counselor.

He has given his time to volunteer at Northeast Vermont Regional Hospital, The Hudson Valley Rapture Center, and the Nature Zone, an educational exotic animal park in Lynchburg, VA. For ten years he was a regular volunteer during the summer months at various spiritual communities. He served the wellness center at Omega Institute in Rhinebeck, NY and assisted with mountain retreats at The Abode of the Message in New Lebanon, NY. He has also been a volunteer at Satchidananda Ashram in Buckingham, Virginia.

I hope that my book touched you in some way. If it did, I am asking that you contact me and share the details. Nowadays, a book is usually a stepping stone to something more grandiose. I believe The Cosmic Guru or Swan Song book has great potential to be adapted into a movie. I am seeking a spiritual-based organization to produce this movie. Contact me if you want to sponsor *The Movie* or would like to be updated about the progress.

My spiritual journey ultimately led to establishing the Cristo Morpho Volunteer Program and Cristo Morpho Community. We are located on nearly one hundred acres of rain forest in the mountain village of Buena Vista on the Caribbean side of Costa Rica. I am seeking individuals, families or a spiritual organization that would like to establish their own community or assist in taking our community to the next level. The fruit trees, vegetable gardens, and hardwood trees on our land have been designated to serve the needs of a medium-sized community. This rainforest location is a perfect place to offer spiritual retreats.

We need pioneers willing to commit their time and energy. Perhaps it is your desire to help preserve the rainforest or reduce your stress level by getting back to Nature. Part of our vision is to fulfill the dreams of individuals and families that resonate with our core values. They include respect toward all people and cultures, honoring family and relationships, and living a healthy drug-free lifestyle. Please contact me if you desire to become actively involved in a sustainable community. I am here to serve you.

May peace be with you,

Randolph C. Phelps
P.O. Box 255, Danville, VT 05828
cristomorpho@gmail.com
www.cristomorpho.com

www.ingramcontent.com/pod-product-compliance
Lightning Source LLC
Chambersburg PA
CBHW031547040426
42452CB00006B/220